[In their] wealth there is a known share for the beggars and the destitute (70:24-25)

Zakāt Calculation

Primarily Based on *Fiqh uz-Zakāt* by Yūsuf al-Qaraḍāwī

Mushfiqur Rahman

THE ISLAMIC FOUNDATION

Published by

THE ISLAMIC FOUNDATION,

Markfield Conference Centre,
Ratby Lane, Markfield, Leicester LE67 9SY, UK
Tel: (01530) 244944, Fax: (01530) 244946
E-mail: info@islamic-foundation.org.uk
Web site: http://www.islamic-foundation.org.uk

Quran House, PO Box 30611, Nairobi, Kenya

PMB 3193, Kano, Nigeria

British Library Cataloguing-in-Publication Data
Rahman, Mushfiqur
Zakat Calculation: primarily based on fiqh uz-Zakat
by Yusuf al-Qaradawi
1. Qaradawi, Yusuf. Fiqh uz-Zakat
2. Zakat
I. Title
297.5'4

ISBN 0–86037–388–6

Typeset by: N.A. Qaddoura
Cover design: Nasir Cadir

Sayyid Abu'l A'lā Mawdūdī

Whose simple, clear, and yet powerful strokes of pen have cleared away many misconceptions in my mind and helped me re-discover Islam in its original beauty.

Transliteration Table

Consonants. Arabic

initial: unexpressed medial and final:

ء	ʼ	د	d	ض	ḍ	ك	k
ب	b	ذ	dh	ط	ṭ	ل	l
ت	t	ر	r	ظ	ẓ	م	m
ث	th	ز	z	ع	ʻ	ن	n
ج	j	س	s	غ	gh	هـ	h
ح	ḥ	ش	sh	ف	f	و	w
خ	kh	ص	ṣ	ق	q	ي	y

Vowels, diphthongs, etc.

Short:	ـَ a	ـِ i	ـُ u
long:	ـَا ā	ـِي ī	ـُو ū
diphthongs:		ـَوْ aw	
		ـَيْ ay	

بسم الله الرحمن الرحيم

Contents

Foreword

The Islamic Foundation took the lead in introducing and promoting the cause of Islamic Economics in English and other European languages in the West. It organized International Conferences and Seminars in collaboration with the Islamic Development Bank, Saudi Arabia, International Association for Islamic Economics, and Department of Economics, Loughborough University, UK. In addition, its publications on Islamic Economics, around fifty so far, have gone a long way in familiarizing many with the theory and practice of Islamic Economics.

It is therefore our pleasure to bring out Mr. Mushfiqur Rahman's *Zakāt Calculation: Primarily Based on Fiqh uz-Zakāt by Yūsuf al-Qaraḍāwī*. This helpful guide is intended to clarify important points about zakāt and enable readers to work out their zakāt, which is to be paid as an important Islamic obligation. Mr. Rahman has ably covered all the relevant issues, bringing home the importance of Zakāt, its conditions and the main principles to be followed in assessing Zakāt. His discussion on disbursing Zakāt is equally perceptive and helpful. The forms for calculating Zakāt are both instructive and comprehensive. We are sure readers will find this guidebook useful and will favour us with their comments and suggestions. It would help the author and the Foundation to improve the work further.

August 2003
Jumādā al-Thānī 1424 H

M. Manazir Ahsan
Director General

Introduction

The Need for a Calculation Form

Zakāt is the third pillar of Islam, which comes immediately after *ṣalāt* and before *ṣiyām* and *ḥajj*. Yet, it is the least understood of the five pillars. It is an unfortunate fact that many Muslims do not know how to properly calculate their zakāt. There are some who underpay zakāt because of not assessing their zakāt correctly and there are others who do not pay zakāt despite maintaining a lavish life-style – due to the consideration that they do not owe zakāt since they do not retain any savings at the end of the year. And there are those who are simply frustrated about how to calculate zakāt and so pay only an arbitrary amount to absolve themselves of the obligation.

This should be a great concern for us considering the fact that Islam puts a tremendous emphasis on helping the disadvantaged sector of our society – the poor and the needy – in order to maintain a just, equitable, and compassionate society. It is also embarrassing, especially in the Western societies where Muslims find themselves in a position to explain Islam to the non-Muslims and the Muslim converts, that a pillar as important as zakāt remains to be little or not understood.

It should, therefore, be considered a priority task for the scholars to develop zakāt calculation forms that will help zakāt payers to properly and easily assess their zakāt according to the *sharīʿa* and without any confusion. There is also a need to prepare easy-to-read booklets that will explain the concept of zakāt to the ordinary Muslim population. Both of these priorities can be addressed together in the same work, which is what we have attempted in this book.

A Critical Look at the Existing Forms

During the last few years, some zakāt calculation forms have been made available by a few Islamic and charitable organizations. These efforts deserve appreciation and they will one day lead to the development of more accurate forms. However, in these existing forms we observe certain limitations, which include:

- Not factoring in *niṣāb* in the assessment of zakātable assets.
- Imposing zakāt irrespective of wealth needed to fulfill the essential needs of the zakāt payer.
- Confusion of what is *niṣāb* as defined in the *sharīʿa* with what is needed to satisfy basic needs.
- Combining all forms of assets together and then comparing the total value with *niṣāb*.
- No consideration for debts of the zakāt payer.
- No consideration for loans owed to the zakāt payer.
- Not imposing zakāt on earnings, such as wages and salaries.

- Not calculating or incorrect calculation of business assets and income, or confusion about trading goods and fixed assets.
- Incorrect application, or non-application, of the *passage of a year*.
- Imposing zakāt on jewelry regardless of customary or personal use.
- Potential for duplication of zakāt in the same year.

Essential Elements of a Zakāt Form

A zakāt calculation form must conform to the *sharīʿa*. When the *sharīʿa* provides a clear principle in the calculation of zakāt, that principle cannot be violated or ignored. It is surprising that some existing forms do not consider the *niṣāb*, which in *sharīʿa* is a primary factor in the calculation of zakāt. Similarly, some forms do not include deduction of debt when almost all scholars agree on its deduction. Equally objectionable is the position that the methodology of zakāt calculation should be revised in our modern time, such as in the rate of *niṣāb* and how it is applied, despite having clear texts and guidelines in the *Sunna* of the Prophet (peace be upon him) regarding *niṣāb* on various assets. Maḥmūd Abū Saʿūd writes in his *Contemporary Zakāt*: "*It is not an exaggeration to say that most of those who specialized in Islamic Sciences have become obstacles in the road to progress and evolution simply because they insist upon the application of old legislation and obsolete rules in our contemporary societies which hardly bear any resemblance to the past activities.*" He further remarks, "*The evolution of human civilizations has gone so far that little resemblance to the past remains.*" Consequently, he argues that "*the evaluation of*

Zakāt and Zakātable wealth are subject to change according to the public interest in different communities."[1]

With respect, we differ. To consider that modern life has little resemblance with that of the past is, in our view, both an oversimplification of the past life and an exaggeration of the modern life. True, we now fly in airplanes to commute from one place to another as opposed to riding camels, or live in high-rise apartment complexes as opposed to mud huts, or drive to shining supermarkets and pay for commodities using "plastic money" (credit card) as opposed to walking to the crowded bazaars and pay using silver or gold coins or simply by barter. But such extraneous and visual elements in life are not what matters in the calculation of zakāt. Life with all its basic complexities has remained the same. Life has been highly civilized and organized since much earlier than the time of the Prophet (peace be upon him) and his Companions. They did trade, engaged in commercial transactions, did deals and reached agreements, ran business enterprises and employed staff, took and disbursed loans, rented properties, calculated profit and loss, devised laws and regulations, used currency in payment for goods and services, and engaged in an array of other activities that an organized life require. To think that their society was primitive and without the complexities of civilization is utterly simplistic. Instead, it was a highly civilized and organized society containing people of various professions and of characters from the pious and righteous to atheists and criminals. They had a system of law, order, and a judicial proceedings. They governed cities and provinces; they dealt with and resolved societal and citizen issues. Education was highly valued and they excelled in poetry and literature. One can go on and on, but the point is that life in its core and essential complexities has not much changed since the time of the Prophet (peace be upon him), certainly not to the extent that renders the text involving zakāt calculation obsolete. God forbid, that cannot be the case for the Divine religion, much less for one of its basic pillars. To argue that the zakāt calculation method that the Law Giver provided is not going to work in our time is to question the universality of the religion itself.

Designing a zakāt calculation form that adequately addresses modern forms of assets, financial services, earnings and other contemporary issues requires making *ijtihād* in different areas. That, however, should be carefully done in the light of the *sharīʿa* without violating an established principle. We, therefore, subscribe to the view that the respected scholar Yūsuf al-Qaraḍāwī expressed in the following words, which is in line with the view of other contemporary scholars including Sayyid Mawdūdī:

[Ash-Shāṭibī says] that in transactions that have some characteristics of worship, we should limit ourselves to the texts. This applies not only to *zakāt* but also to the requirements of *ṣadāq* (dowry) in marriage, the distribution of shares in inheritance, the number of months women wait in *ʿidda* (the waiting period after divorce or being widowed), etc. I add to these the percentages of *zakāt* and its *niṣāb* (minimum) because these are issues clearly defined by texts and on which Muslims never disagree. So it is essential to abide by these texts and this *ijmāʿ*. For this reason I disagree with those who claim that the minimum exemption and rates of *zakāt* are subject to change according to changing circumstances in time and place, on the grounds that such changes conform to the objectives and common benefits of *zakāt*. I believe such changes alter the features of *zakāt* and reduce it to a mere civil tax, like other taxes imposed by governments.[2]

The second element of the form should be its easiness and clarity so that the zakāt payer is not left with confusion in following the form or calculating zakāt using the form. However, too simple a form may not correctly and adequately address many contemporary issues. For a form to calculate zakāt accurately and to be useful to most zakāt payers, it has to address certain details. But it should provide sufficient instructions to help the zakāt payer in using the form and following its calculations. Finally, for a form to gain the acceptance and confidence of zakāt payers, it should provide texts and discussions that back the calculations, especially when an issue is debatable or is not easily understood by most individuals.

Why *Fiqh uz-Zakāt*?

Al-Qaraḍāwī[3] has done a great service to the Muslim *umma* by providing his monumental work, *Fiqh uz-Zakāt*. In this 750-page work (English translation), he does a very detailed and elaborate treatment of many contemporary issues and topics related to zakāt. On a given topic, he first describes the opinions of all major scholars *from their point of view* before providing his comprehensive analysis and opinion, something that is typical of al-Qaraḍāwī. In his analysis he is open-minded and free from any *madhhab* affiliations. He accepts the opinion of any scholar – whether classical or modern –

if he finds that to be closer to the *sharīʿa* or the spirit of the *sharīʿa*. Where he provides his own opinion, he does so after providing sufficient argument for it in his usual convincing manner in the light of the *sharīʿa*. Such a comprehensive work on zakāt is invaluable, especially since it is the least understood of the pillars of Islam and little has been written on it by modern scholars in light of modern issues.

We have, therefore, based our work primarily on *Fiqh uz-Zakāt*. Although *Fiqh us-Sunna* by the late scholar as-Sayyid Sābiq and other works on zakāt have been consulted and examined, most of the opinions expressed in this work are taken from *Fiqh uz-Zakāt* and references have been provided so that the reader may acquire a more detailed understanding of the issue at hand by checking *Fiqh uz-Zakāt* and other materials from where we have quoted. Rarely have we expressed our own opinion, and that is done only when an opinion by al-Qaraḍāwī and other experts was not available or was not clear or we have not found a suitable solution to the issue at hand. In that case, the text points out whom the opinion belongs to.

Note to the Zakāt Payer

Finally, there is no claim that this work is devoid of error or the opinions expressed by the author are *fiqhī* opinions to the calibre of a legal expert. It is only a sincere and humble effort to help one calculate zakāt according to the *sharīʿa*. Everyone is urged to develop an understanding of the principles of zakāt assessment based on the authentic sources so that he/she is able to calculate zakāt as accurately as possible.

If anyone has any questions or needs consultation in calculating zakāt, then he or she should feel free to contact us at *mushfiqurrahman@hotmail.com*.

On Allah I rely and to Him I shall return to account for my deeds.

Reston, USA
June 30, 2003

Mushfiqur Rahman

Notes

1. Mahmūd Abū Sa'ūd, *Contemporary Zakāt*, Zakāt and Research Foundation, Indianapolis, 1988, pp. 19-20, 24.

2. Yūsuf al-Qaraḍāwī, *Fiqh uz-Zakāt: A Comparative Study*, Dar al-Taqwa Ltd., London, 1999, p. xxxviii.

3. Yūsuf al-Qaraḍāwī is one of the most respected and well-known scholars of our time. He was born in Egypt in 1926. Before his 10th birthday, he completed memorization of the Qur'ān. He later studied at Al-Azhar and from there obtained his Ph.D in 1973. He currently lives in Qatar where he serves as the dean of the College of Sharī'ah and Islamic Studies and as the director of the Center for Sunnah and Sirah Studies at the University of Qatar. He has authored over forty books. Among the works that have been translated into English are *The Lawful and the Prohibited in Islam*, *Islamic Awakening between Rejection and Extremism*, *Priorities of the Islamic Movement in the Coming Phase*, and *Fiqh uz-Zakāt*.

CHAPTER ❖ 1

Importance of Zakāt

Zakāt is the Third Pillar of Islam

Zakāt is one of the five pillars of Islam on which stands the structure of Islam. Some people erroneously think that the place of zakāt comes after *ṣiyām* (fasting), or even *ḥajj* (pilgrimage). Zakāt is actually the third pillar of Islam that comes immediately after *ṣalat* (prayer). Its importance can be realized from the fact that in eighty-two verses of the Qur'ān zakāt is associated with *ṣalāt*, such as:

> Establish regular Prayer and give zakāt. (73:20)
>
> Establish regular Prayer and give zakāt; and obey Allah and His Messenger. (33:33)
>
> Be steadfast in Prayer; give zakāt, and bow down your heads with those who bow down. (2:43)

If social justice and compassion to fellow humans who are disadvantaged is one of the central themes in the message of Allah (swt) to humanity, then it is no wonder that zakāt, like *ṣalāt* and *ṣiyām*, was also enjoined upon the people of the past messengers:

> And We made them (descendants of Abraham) leaders, guiding by Our Command, and We sent them inspiration to do good deeds, to establish regular Prayers and to practise zakāt; and they constantly served Us. (21:73)

> Also mention in the Book (the story of) Ishmael: he was (strictly) true to what he promised, and he was a messenger (and) a prophet. He used to enjoin on his people Prayer and Zakāt, and he was most acceptable in the sight of his Lord. (19:54-55)

> And remember We took a covenant from the Children of Israel: Worship none but Allah; treat with kindness your parents and kindred, and orphans and those in need; speak fair to the people; be steadfast in Prayer and practise Zakāt. (2:83)

> [Jesus] said: "I am indeed a servant of Allah: He has given me revelation and made me a prophet; and He has made me blessed wheresoever I be, and has enjoined on me Prayer and Zakāt as long as I live." (19:30-31)

Reference to tithe[4] can also be seen in the Old Testament where it is mentioned:

> Bring ye all the tithes into the storehouse, that there may be meat in mine house, and prove me now herewith, saith the Lord of the hosts ... (Malachi 3:10)

This verse is used by the Church of Jesus Christ of Latter-Day Saints (the Mormons) as support for requiring tithe on its followers, which they faithfully oblige.[5]

Zakāt is obligatory on one who has wealth that reaches or exceeds a certain level called the *niṣāb*. Unlike tax, however, zakāt is an act of worship for which one receives reward from Allah (swt).[6] Ignoring to pay zakāt, on the other hand, is a major sin. According to the scholars, anyone who does not pay zakāt by denying its obligation is considered a disbeliever.[7]

Zakāt is the Right of the Poor

Zakāt is not considered a favour that is given to the poor by the rich. It is the right of the poor on the wealth of the rich. Allah (swt) says:

> [In their] wealth there is a known share for the beggars and the destitute. (70:24-25)

Zakāt, therefore, is unlike charity that is given to the needy voluntarily. Withholding zakāt is considered depriving the poor of their due share. Thus one who pays zakāt actually "purifies" his wealth by separating from it the portion that belongs to the poor.

If One Dies Before Paying Zakāt

Since zakāt is the right of the poor on the wealth of the rich, death of a wealthy person does not absolve him of the obligation of unpaid zakāt. According to imāms ash-Shāfiʿī, Aḥmad, and Sābiq, if one dies before paying zakāt then the unpaid zakāt must be taken out from his estate and paid to the poor before the estate is distributed among his heirs.[8] Bukhārī and Muslim report the following *ḥadīth* regarding this:

> A man came to the Messenger of Allah, upon whom be peace, and said: "My mother died while she still had to make up one month of fasting. Shall I make it up for her?" The Prophet replied, "If there was any debt upon your mother, would you pay it off for her?" The man answered: "Yes". The Prophet then observed: "A debt to Allah is more deserving to be paid off."

It should be mentioned in this context the case where zakāt is lost before it is distributed, such as due to calamities, neglect, or otherwise. It is agreed upon that if zakāt is delayed after harvesting is done and subsequently the harvest is damaged before zakāt is paid on it, then that does not absolve the owner of the crop of paying zakāt that was due based on the original harvest. According to some the zakāt remains due *"whether the loss occurred owing to negligence or not."*[9] In that case, zakāt becomes a debt that must be paid even if the owner does not have sufficient money to pay it. According to this opinion, even if one sets aside the zakāt and then it is lost, the obligation to pay remains since it is still the responsibility of the zakāt payer to disburse it, says Sābiq who quotes the following report narrated by Ibn Ḥazm:

> Whoever sets aside zakāt from his property and then it is lost, his obligation to pay zakāt still remains to be discharged, and he must set aside again.[10]

According to other jurists, zakāt liability remains in case of loss or damage of the due zakāt only if the delay of zakāt payment was due to negligence and not to any valid and justifiable cause.

This discussion brings home one very important point: zakāt is a serious business in the *sharīʿa*. As soon as it is due on one's wealth, that portion of the wealth belongs to the poor who is now considered its rightful owner. One, therefore, should not feel comfortable with any zakāt amount that has not yet been distributed. After all, which God-fearing Muslim can sleep at night without a guarantee that he will wake up the next morning to distribute his unpaid zakāt?

Punishment for Not Paying Zakāt

One who incurs zakāt and yet does not pay it will receive severe punishment in the Hereafter. Allah (swt) says in the Qur'ān:

> ... those who hoard treasures of gold and silver and do not spend them for the sake of Allah – warn them of grievous sufferings (on the Day of Judgment). On that day when (the hoarded wealth) shall be heated in the Fires of Hell and their foreheads and their sides and their backs branded with it (it will be said to them), "These are the treasures which you have hoarded for yourselves. Now taste of what you used to accumulate!" (9: 34-35)

In a *ḥadīth*, the Prophet (peace be upon him) said:

> If someone is given wealth by Allah but does not pay its zakāt, that wealth will appear to him on the Day of Judgment in the form of a bald serpent with two horns, encircling him and squeezing him all day, then holding him by the lips and telling him, "I am your wealth, your treasure which you hoarded".[11]

In addition to receiving punishment in the Hereafter for not paying zakāt and thus depriving the poor of their rights, the individual may also incur loss in his wealth and property or face some other forms of calamity in this world. The Prophet (peace be upon him) said:

> Whenever any amount of wealth is destroyed in the land or in the sea it could be because its zakāt was not paid.[12]

In another *ḥadīth*, the Prophet (peace be upon him) said:

> Zakāt is never intermingled with any amount of wealth without destroying and rotting it.[13]

Thus, one may face punishment both in this world and the Hereafter for not paying zakāt. But the better person is indeed he or she who pays zakāt not for fear of punishment but out of compassion towards those who are needy and out of being grateful to Allah (swt) for blessing him or her to be the one among those who are zakāt givers and not of those who are zakāt receivers.

Effects of Zakāt on Individuals

Zakāt benefits not only the one who receives it but also the zakāt payer himself. Al-Qaraḍāwī and other scholars described the beneficial effects that zakāt brings to the individual and his wealth. In brief, these effects are:

Zakāt as a Reminder that Wealth Belongs to Allah
In several verses where Allah (swt) commands the believers to pay zakāt, He uses the phrase "*And give of what We have given them*". "*This implies*", says Sayyid Quṭb,

"the believers' inner belief that what they own and possess is a gift and favour from God. It is not of their own making."[14] That belief is reflected when a Muslim voluntarily and with gratitude pays a small portion of his wealth as zakāt as he is reminded that his entire wealth is a gift from Allah.

Zakāt Purifies the Soul from Miserliness

When one pays zakāt from his wealth, he gives up part of his wealth to help the poor and the needy. Such an act is contrary to greed and love of material wealth. Thus zakāt purifies the soul and removes miserliness.

Zakāt Trains One to Give

By paying zakāt every year, one develops a regular habit of giving and helping the poor. It is likely that this will become a permanent quality and he will continue to help those in need with zakāt and charity.

Zakāt Trains One to Acquire Divine Characteristics

One of Allah's divine characteristics is absolute mercy. By giving zakāt and helping the destitute, one develops mercy and compassion towards others, and his soul is elevated above the lowly animal nature of covetousness.

Zakāt as an Expression of Thankfulness to Allah

By paying zakāt out of submission to Allah, one expresses his thanks and gratitude to Allah for the material bounty that He has given him. For it is Allah Who makes one poor or rich. Imām al-Ghazālī says that one offers thanks to Allah for the bounties of creation (such as health) by praying, and he shows thanks to Allah for the bounties of material wealth by paying zakāt on it.[15]

Zakāt is a Cure for the Love of Worldly Things

Accumulation of wealth enables one to spend it for worldly enjoyments and material objects. The nature of material attraction, says Muhammad Asad, is such that once an object is acquired, the goal is then set to get another object that would bring new satisfaction to the mind.[16] This is an endless cycle that can make one forget the life of the Hereafter. Zakāt helps one break that cycle, for when paying zakāt one spends money that brings no material benefit to him.

Zakāt Stimulates Personality Growth

By paying zakāt, one gets a sense of satisfaction for both performing an *ʿibādah* and for being able to help others. This can increase his self-esteem and enable him to grow as an individual.

Zakāt Improves Ties of Mutual Love

People love those who do good to them. Zakāt makes the poor appreciate the rich for their giving and pray for them while it makes the rich show a concern for the poor. Thus zakāt bonds the two parties together and increases their mutual appreciation.

Zakāt Purifies Wealth

Zakāt is the right of the poor and it belongs to them. If it is not paid and is left mixed with the wealth of the owner, then it can make his wealth rotten according to the *ḥadīth* mentioned before. Allah (swt) says:

> Take charity from their wealth in order to purify and sanctify them. (9:103)

And said the Prophet (peace be upon him):

> Pay zakāt out of your property, for truly it is a purifier which purifies you, and be kind to your relatives, and acknowledge the rights of the poor, neighbours, and beggars.[17]

Zakāt is also a debt to the poor until it is paid, and debt usually brings anxiety. In addition, a good servant of Allah will not feel comfortable with his wealth while there are many who are less fortunate and live in miserable conditions. By allowing part of the wealth to be distributed among the poor, zakāt purifies the wealth as it also purifies the mind of the payer.

Zakāt Brings Growth to Wealth

Zakāt may seem to reduce wealth, but in fact it brings blessings and prosperity to wealth. Allah (swt) is the Giver of wealth and He can increase it for whomever He wants:

> [Allah] enlarges and restricts the Sustenance to such of His servants as He pleases, and nothing do you spend in the least (in His cause) but He replaces it, for He is the Best of Providers. (34:39)

The Prophet (peace be upon him) said:

> I swear upon three (things) and ask you to memorize my words: charity taken from a property never decreases it; a man who suffers injustice and is patient with it, Allah will grant him strength; a man who starts begging, Allah will cause him to be poor.[18]
>
> Wealth never decreases due to charity.[19]

On the contrary, miserliness and non-payment of zakāt can deprive one of the blessings of Allah on his wealth and consequently make him sustain loss or calamity.

These are some of the many benefits that zakāt brings both to the individual and his wealth. Indeed, the very root word from which the term "zakāt" is derived means "to increase", "to purify", and "to bless", all of which are realized when one pays zakāt.

Building a Zakāt-Conscious Society

> The believers, men and women, are protectors of one another: they enjoin what is just and forbid what is evil; they observe regular prayer and practise Zakāt, and obey Allah and His Messenger. On them will Allah pour His Mercy: for Allah is Exalted in Power, Wise. (9:71)

Mention of zakāt in the above verse is significant, which points out the characteristics of an ideal community in which its members care for one another; deal justly with each other and refrain from hurting others; who look forward to the opportunity to pay zakāt to those in need and hold supreme the commands of Allah and His Messenger. Its members are in a bond of mutual love and sympathy helping each other out in times of need. Zakāt plays a key role in bringing about such an ideal society, for it not only helps the needy and allows an ongoing circulation and distribution of capital from the rich to the poor sectors of the community, but at the same time it builds a relationship of compassion and appreciation between one another among its members.

If zakāt helps in bringing about such a society, can we then transform our society into one where everyone takes zakāt as seriously as tax returns and eagerly looks forward to calculating it at the end of the zakāt year? Can we re-establish zakāt again as a pillar in our day-to-day practice of Islam following the early Madinan society?

If such a society is to emerge again, then it must begin with each one of us – except those who are obviously the zakāt receivers – developing a habit of filling up a zakāt calculation form every year. Even those who are not sure that zakāt is due on them should fill up a form to see if they owe any zakāt, just as most of us prepare tax returns every year regardless of whether we owe taxes or not. Whether one uses a zakāt calculation form or uses his own independent method of determining zakāt, and whether one's zakātable assets come out to be above or below *niṣāb*, he should keep records of his calculation worksheets every year. This will help one develop a regular habit of calculating zakāt every year. In addition, past years' zakāt calculation records will enable one to re-assess his zakāt for a previous year if that becomes necessary, such as due to new revelations or mistakes.

"Have you prepared your tax return yet?" – if this question is taken without any offence, then so should be the question, "I calculated my zakāt last weekend. Have you done yours?", especially during the month of Ramaḍān. Sayyid Mawdūdī said that Muslims should do voluntary *ʿibādah* (worship) secretly because those are done exclusively for Allah (swt), but they should do their obligatory acts openly so that others are reminded to do theirs. To build a zakāt-conscious society, such reminding by one another will be instrumental.

We must also teach our children who own zakātable wealth to calculate their zakāt on a regular basis. Whether or not they owe zakāt the children should fill up a zakāt calculation form every year, if not to pay zakāt then to develop a habit. Since their living expenses are provided for by their parents, many children likely possess sufficient amounts of money or wealth that reach or exceed *niṣāb*, making zakāt due on them. It is the responsibility of the parents to teach their children the importance of zakāt and help them calculate it. They should also encourage their children to keep their zakāt calculation records for future reference.

Zakāt is incumbent on every Muslim possessing wealth, whether adult or minor. By each individual becoming serious about calculating zakāt every year routinely at a specific time and encouraging others to do the same, he or she will help bring about a society that can be truly called a "zakāt-conscious society", a society reminiscent of the early Madinan community in its seriousness in paying, collecting and distributing zakāt.

Notes

4. *Tithe* is one tenth of one's land produce or income that is given as religious tax.

5. According to Gordon B. Hinckley, President of the Mormon Church. See www.mormons.org/question/faq

6. Sayyid Quṭb, *In the Shade of the Qur'ān*, Vol. IV, The Islamic Foundation, Leicester, 2001, p. 161.

7. As-Sayyid Sābiq, *Fiqh us-Sunna*, American Trust Publications, Indianapolis, 1991, Vol. III, p. 7; *Fiqh uz-Zakāt*, p. 35.

8. *Fiqh us-Sunna*, p. 10.

9. *ibid.*, p. 55.

10. *ibid.*, p. 56.

11. Reported by al-Bukhārī.

12. Reported by aṭ-Ṭabarānī in *al-Awsaṭ*. Cited by al-Qaraḍāwī, p. 29.

13. Reported by al-Bazzār and al-Bayhaqī in *at-Targhīb*, by ash-Shāfiʿī in *at-Muntaqā*, and by al-Bukhārī in *History*. Cited by al-Qaraḍāwī, p. 28.

14. *In the Shade of the Qur'ān*, Vol. I, p. 24. To elaborate the point: If one thinks that his wealth and fortune is a result of his own labour and talent, then that reflects a serious lack of understanding and insight on his or her part. While there is no denial that one should put efforts towards achieving his goal as Islam requires and as the Prophet (peace be upon him) himself did, but to think that utilization of one's talent and exerting his labour alone earned him his wealth is to deny both facts as well as to betray common sense observation. There are many around us who with greater talents and more efforts fail to "succeed" in life and reach "financial security". And there are those who within moments lose their vast fortunes, or suddenly become rich, due to market fluctuation, calamity, unforeseen business deals, or otherwise. And finally, there are always these basic questions to ask: Who is the One Who provided him with his talents and abilities? Who has provided him with that particular set of resources that he successfully utilized and which others were not provided with? Who controls the events that occur in our day-to-day life and Who provided those particular chances and deals that contributed to his fortune? Wise people know the answers to these questions and, consequently, humble themselves and thank Allah (swt) for His favour.

15. *Fiqh uz-Zakāt*, p. 541.

16. *"... at no time before this had greed outgrown a mere eagerness to acquire things and become an obsession that blurred the sight of everything else; an irresistible craving to get, to do, to contrive more and more – more today than yesterday, and more tomorrow than today: a demon riding on the necks of men and whipping their hearts forward toward goals that tauntingly glitter in the distance but dissolve into contemptible nothingness as soon as they are reached, always holding out the promise of new goals ahead – goals still more brilliant, more tempting as long as they lie on the horizon, and bound to wither into further nothingness as soon as they come within grasp ..."* – Muhammad Asad, *The Road To Mecca*, The Muslim Academic Trust, 1998, p. 310. First published in 1954 by Simon & Schuster, New York.

17. Reported by Aḥmad.
18. Reported by al-Tirmidhī.
19. Reported by Muslim.

CHAPTER ❖ 2

Conditions of Zakātability

Assets Subject to Zakāt

- The asset should be of a growing type or should have the potential for growth, such as money, livestock, property, etc. These are called growing assets since they have the potential to grow or generate income.
- One full lunar year should pass since the ownership of the wealth for zakāt to be due. This condition is restricted to livestock, money (money as saved assets; not wages, professional income, etc.), and business assets. It does not include crops, fruits, minerals, earned income, and treasure.[20]
- The asset must be at or above a certain limit called the *niṣāb*. *Sharīʿa* defines different *niṣāb* for different types of assets.
- The assets should be in excess of basic needs. What is needed by an individual to satisfy the basic necessities for him and his family is not subject to zakāt.

- The asset must be lawfully and completely owned.
- Debt reduces zakātable assets by the amount of the debt. If debt exceeds the asset or brings its worth to below *niṣāb*, zakāt is not due.

People Subject to Zakāt

- Zakāt is imposed only on Muslims. Non-Muslim citizens of an Islamic state are not subject to zakāt.
- Zakātability is a condition on wealth regardless of whether it is owned by an adult or a minor. Therefore, zakāt is due on wealth owned by minors and the insane as well. This is the view of the Companions ʿUmar, ʿAlī, ʿĀ'isha, Ibn ʿUmar and Jābir, and Imāms Aḥmad, ash-Shāfiʿī, and Mālik. This is also the view of Sābiq and al-Qaraḍāwī.[21] Legal guardians should pay zakāt on behalf of the minor or the insane.
- There is no zakāt on Muslim converts for the past period of disbelief.[22]

Notes

20. *Fiqh uz-Zakāt*, pp. 96, 98-99.
21. *Fiqh us-Sunna*, p. 9; *Fiqh uz-Zakāt*, p. 57.
22. *Fiqh uz-Zakāt*, p. 42.

CHAPTER ❖ 3

Basic Principles of Assessing Zakāt

Contrary to what many people may realize, the rules of zakāt assessment on various types of assets are bound by certain underlying principles, which point to the great wisdom of the Law Giver. These principles are excellently brought to light by al-Qaraḍāwī and other contemporary jurists. Therefore, when deriving at or criticizing the method and rate of zakāt on a particular type of asset, one must keep in mind these overall principles and make sure that the particular ruling fits within those principles.

For example, when fixed assets are used to generate growth, zakāt is assessed on the growth only and the fixed asset itself is exempted from zakāt. On the growth, zakāt is assessed at the rate of 10% of the net income or 5% of the gross income. Based on that principle, zakāt is not assessed on agricultural land but on the growth of the land (i.e., the crop) at the rate of 10% on the net income (i.e., watered by rain, and thus the expenses are covered). Based on that same principle, buildings are exempted from zakāt but their growth (i.e., rent) is subjected to zakāt at the rate of 10% of the net income. Now, if one proposes that the rate should be 2.5%, then there will be an obvious discrepancy between zakāt on agricultural land and zakāt on rental buildings. Likewise, considering that zakāt cannot be assessed on earnings until one full year has passed from the day it was earned practically reduces zakātability to savings that are kept for one year, thus eliminating other sources of earnings from zakāt such as rent and business income.

When the overall principles of zakāt are realized and kept in mind, one will appreciate the wisdom behind the laws of zakāt that the Law Giver has provided and will develop a comprehensive understanding where all the pieces regarding zakātability on various types of assets will fit together within those broad principles.

With this introduction, we now discuss below the assessment of zakāt on various types of assets.

Agricultural Output

Agricultural produce, such as grains are zakātable. According to Abū Ḥanīfa, ʿUmar ibn ʿAbdul-ʿAzīz, Mujāhid and al-Qaraḍāwī, other agricultural produce, such as fruits and vegetables are also zakātable. Zakāt is 10% if the land is watered by rain all or most of the year, and 5% if it is watered by irrigation all or most of the year. If the land is watered by rain half of the year, then zakāt is 7.5%.[23]

The majority of the scholars agree that *niṣāb* on crops is five *wasaqs*, which is equivalent to 653 kilograms according to al-Qaraḍāwī. *Wasaq*, however was used as a measurement of volume. But any crop that is usually measured in weight, 653 kg should be the *niṣāb* for it. According to al-Qaraḍāwī, for crops that are not measured in weight, a fair *niṣāb* should be decided upon by each country based on 5 *wasaqs* of an average grain and socio-economic and other variables. But that estimation of *niṣāb* should be fair to both the zakāt payer and the poor.[24]

Agricultural Land

There is no zakāt on the value of agricultural land but only on the growth that the land generates, i.e., the harvest. But if the land is rented to a farmer, then the farmer pays zakāt on the crop while the owner pays zakāt on the rent he receives. In that sense, both land and crop is subject to zakāt. All associated expenses, including real estate taxes, may be deducted from the rent income. Zakāt is 10% of the net income or 5% of the gross income, depending on the method that is used on the output itself.[25]

Business Goods and Business Income

There are two kinds of assets for the purpose of zakāt calculation: (1) trading goods, and (2) exploited assets.

Trading goods are assets that are obtained for resale, such as business inventory. They also include land, house, buildings, furniture, clothing, foodstuff, machinery, jewelry, livestock, etc. if these are obtained for resale. Zakāt on them is 2.5% of the appraised value if it reaches the *niṣāb,* which is the value of 85 grams of gold. Livestock also fall in this category, although their zakāt and *niṣāb* is different. When appraising the value of the goods, only those should be included that have been kept for one lunar year.

Zakāt on business goods can be calculated by adding the following together: (1) Appraised value of all merchandise and trade goods that are kept for a lunar year (2) Cash in hand and in bank and (3) Money that customers owe to the business and is expected to be paid back. From the total sum, subtract debts and expenses. If the balance reaches *niṣāb* then zakāt is 2.5% on the balance. If this is the only income of the zakāt payer, then *niṣāb* should be calculated after deducting basic needs for the family.[26]

For retail businesses, a difficulty may arise in determining the trading goods that have been kept for one year due to the short life span of the inventoried items and the continuous replenishment of the inventory due to ongoing sales. For example, in apparel stores clothing items will continue to be purchased from suppliers and sold to the customers. In such a business, how does one find the clothes that were kept for one year? Our opinion is that the value of the goods prior to the beginning of the zakāt year and at the end of the zakāt year should be determined, and the lesser of the two should be considered the value of the goods that have been kept for one year (see *Determining the Value of a Given Asset* on page 30 for discussion on how to assess the value). This is similar to calculating zakāt on savings (see *Savings* on page 52) and shares and bonds (see *Shares and Bonds* on page 53).

Exploited assets are those that are not obtained for resale but are exploited to generate income. These include fixed business assets, such as buildings, furniture, and fixtures of stores, containers, cages, scales, machinery, etc. This category also includes houses and buildings that are rented. These are not considered trading goods since they are not for resale. Zakāt on this kind of asset is levied on the income that it generates, not on the asset itself.[27] Zakāt is 10% on the net income after deducting all associated expenses including any taxes[28] and amortization,[29] and 5% if calculating on the gross income. (See also *Merchandise* on page 41.)

Converts

There is no zakāt on the assets owned by converts to Islam for the past period of disbelief.[30]

Child Support and Alimony

Our opinion, following the discussion under *Net Earnings vs. Gross Earnings* (see page 44), is that child support and alimony expenses should be deducted from one's earnings if such deduction is required by the law of the land. However, if alimony expenses are deducted from the gross earnings, then the deduction for minimum living expenses should not include expenses for the child since doing that would result in a double deduction. For the calculation of zakāt, such a child should not be considered a dependent of the zakāt payer since he/she is not under the zakāt payer's custody.

Children and The Insane

Zakāt is due on assets even if they are owned by children and the insane, for zakāt is the right of the poor on the wealth of the rich, irrespective of his or her age and sanity. This is the view of Companions ʿUmar, ʿAlī, ʿĀ'isha, Ibn ʿUmar and Jābir, and Imāms Aḥmad, ash-Shāfiʿī, and Mālik, and al-Qaraḍāwī.[31]

Determining the Value of a Given Asset

When assessing zakāt on gold, jewelry, shares, bonds, and trading goods, a question that will arise is: as of what date should the value of these assets be determined? This question is particularly relevant for those types of assets whose value can greatly fluctuate from one period of time to another, such as gold, shares and bonds, and real estate properties.

According to al-Qaraḍāwī and the majority of scholars, current market value as of the due date of zakāt should be used in determining the value of the given asset.[32] This opinion is based on the established principle that zakāt should be calculated and distributed as soon as it is due. For crops, the due date is the day of the harvest and for assets requiring the passage of a year the due date is the last day of the zakāt year. Many jurists agree that if zakāt is not distributed after the due date and then the zakāt amount or the original asset is lost due to any reason, then the zakāt payer still remains obligated to pay the original zakāt amount based on the original asset. (For more discussion on this, see *If One Dies Before Paying Zakāt* on page 11.)

Based on this principle agreed upon by many jurists, Muhammad Majīd, an imām and scholar who provided much valuable input on this work, draws an analogy and argues that shares, bonds, and other assets should be treated in the same way, meaning that the value of the assets in question should be assessed based on their market value as of the due date of zakāt, which will be the last day of the zakāt year for gold, jewelry, trading goods, shares, and bonds. If the owner delays calculating zakāt on the shares he owns and their price meanwhile drops (or rises), then zakāt will still be calculated using their market value as of the zakāt due date.

It should be mentioned here that the form provided at the end of this book for calculating zakāt compares (1) the value of the above assets that the zakāt payer owned on the end date of the last zakāt year per the market value as of that date, with (2) the value of the assets that the zakāt payer owned on the end date of the current zakāt year (for which zakāt is being calculated) per the market value as of that date, in order to determine the value of the asset that has been kept for one year, which will be the lesser of the above two.

Debt

According to most scholars including Imāms Mālik, Aḥmad, and Abū Ḥanīfa, debt prevents zakāt or at least reduces zakāt on the assets by the amount of the outstanding debt. If the owner is burdened by debt that exceeds the *niṣāb* or brings the asset's worth to below *niṣāb*, then zakāt is not due. All debts are, therefore, deductible from assets that are subject to zakāt, according to al-Qaraḍāwī. But debt, to completely waive zakāt, must exceed all assets or bring their worth to below *niṣāb*.[33]

It is surprising that some forms do not consider debts in the calculation of zakāt. According to verse 9:60, one of the categories where zakāt money can be spend is those who are in debt "whether they are employed or unemployed, rich or poor – who would be reduced to a state of poverty if they were to pay off all their debts from the funds available to them."[34] If people in debt are to be helped from the zakāt money, then it implies that one's debts should be deducted from his assets before assessing zakāt.

Can large interest-bearing loans, such as a loan against residential houses and cars be considered deductible debt? Al-Qaraḍāwī does not specifically discuss this in *Fiqh uz-Zakāt*. Our opinion on this is as follows:

1. Housing and shelter is a basic necessity. The justice and fairness of the Islamic Law would dictate that such loans be considered necessary debts that should be deducted from zakātable assets. However, only the capital loan amount should be considered the debt, not the interest amount that is charged on the capital.

2. All payments made should be considered payments towards the capital, although most of the payments usually include interest charges. Payments should therefore reduce the capital debt by the full payment amounts for the purpose of assessing zakāt-exempt debts. This is because interest payments are not recognized as lawful expenditure. Secondly, since a very little part of the monthly payments are applied to the capital, the capital loan is reduced very slowly and therefore remains large and outstanding for as long as 30 years. If payments made are not recognized as fully applied against the capital debt, then this large outstanding debt will make many people exempt from zakāt for many years despite their earning substantial income and living a lavish life-style. This would deprive the poor and the needy from receiving their due share from the wealth of many zakāt payers.

3. The product should be considered a basic necessity. For example, in the presence of a car in good condition that suffices the basic needs for a small family, a second car may not be considered a real necessity and, therefore, any loan on it may not be considered zakāt exempt.

4. The house or the car should be a modest one, and not a lavish or extravagant type. A luxurious house or a car should not be considered a necessity, in our opinion, for debts on such lavish items will prevent zakāt on the income and assets of many rich people.[35] In such cases, only that portion of the loan amount should be considered the "original loan amount" that is below the limit of extravagance. For instance, if one buys a house for $500,000 while the price of a mediocre house is $200,000 in a certain area, then $200,000 should be considered the "loan amount".

Our opinion, therefore, is that loans for housing, car and other necessities can be considered debts for the purpose of calculating zakāt provided that the above requirements are met.

If the last point above raises questions for any who may have purchased an expensive house on loan, then we submit the following for him or her to consider:

a. The full debt on an expensive house or mansion will likely offset most or all zakātable money and assets of the zakāt payer, making him owe no zakāt despite being rich. Since the objective of zakāt is to help the destitute, would it be fair for the *sharīʿa* to deprive the poor of their due share of zakāt in the wealth of the rich because of their extravagant expenses?

b. Ultimately, the rate of zakāt is very small – usually 2.5%. This is a quarter of the religious due that Mormons are required to pay to their church, which is 10%. Since the rate of zakāt is small, it will not likely result in a substantial difference in the zakāt amount even if one argues that the full loan amount should be deducted. For someone who can afford to purchase an expensive house, this small difference will be insignificant compared with many other expenses he normally incurs for himelf and his family. If this difference is indeed difficult for him to pay, then he should not have purchased an expensive house in the first place but should have feared Allah (swt) in spending the money more wisely. We should keep in mind that our money and wealth are but a trust (*amāna*) from Allah. There is much good use for them in this world and we will have to account one day for how and where we spent those valuable resources.

c. Finally, zakāt is for the benefit of the poor. A believer gives it out of gratitude to Allah (swt) for His blessings and out of love and sympathy for the poor. He is, therefore, unlike a contending party in a bargain who is trying to get the most out of the negotiation. Instead, he takes pleasure in giving more to the poor than less.

What is the limit of extravagance? This is a subjective matter and it depends on the type of the amenity or property that one is trying to purchase and the time and place. The zakāt payer should sincerely try to come up with that amount which can purchase a modest property or product that will suffice for his or her family's needs.

Should All Types of Debt be Deductible?

We live in a modern world driven by a culture of consumerism. What used to be once a luxurious item is now considered a need. What is considered a luxury now will become a mere need tomorrow. Thus, the definition of "need" itself is ever changing in our mind. We increasingly find ourselves in "need" of newer products and models that are on the market, thanks to the technological innovations, ever-increasing array of tempting products and services, and industrial marketing campaigns projected at our minds from all corners. If the question of accountability in the Hereafter for the money we spend ever bothers us, then we seek justification for the expenditure we want to commit, and we usually find one quickly. Thus, a substantial part of our earned income is spent in purchasing products and amenities that we would like to have but which are not real necessities.

In such a culture of overwhelming consumerism, it is not unusual for many to have running debts. The question is: should all such debts be deductible?

In our opinion, anyone who understands the spirit of the *sharīʿa* is likely to conclude that only those debts should be deductible that are considered "debt by necessity", as Majīd would like to call it. Debts that occur due to our whims and desires should not be deductible. Deducting such debts would result in a grave injustice to the poor and the needy who are deprived of even the basic necessities of life that we take for granted, such as food, clothing, shelter, transportation, and medical care.

The Issue of Debt: A Balanced Approach

There are some zakāt calculation forms that do not consider deductibility of debts. We have shown above that this is contrary to the opinions of almost all major scholars. On the other hand, some zakāt payers may think that all debts – regardless of how it was incurred or what the limit of modest expense is – should be deductible. This is the other extreme that certainly cannot be the intent of the *sharīʿa* when it allows debts to be deducted.

By deducting only those debts that are "debt by necessity" and by deducting that portion of the debt which is below the level of extravagance, a middle course was adopted. However, a middle course by itself cannot be the objective; our objective was only to implement the intent of the *sharīʿa* which always guides us to the middle course.

An Example for Calculating Debt on a House Loan

Debt calculation due to purchasing residential houses and cars are quite common for many zakāt payers, and hence it would be helpful to illustrate this using an example. Let us assume that someone purchased a house for $200,000. He made a down payment of $10,000 and financed the remaining $190,000.[36] The loan will be repayable in 30 years by paying $1,500 per month (excluding insurance and other charges). Assuming that he has been paying for the last 10 years (120 payments), his remaining debt on the house for the purpose of calculating zakāt will be:

Original loan amount (not to exceed the price of a modest house)	$190,000
Total payments made ($1,500 x 120 months)	- $180,000
Zakāt exempt debt is	$10,000

If he bought the house for a much higher price while $200,000 is the price of a modest house, then the loan amount will still be considered $200,000. Additionally, whether a loan was taken with or without finance charges, all payments will be considered applied against the original loan amount for the purpose of assessing zakāt-exempt debts.

Past Due Zakāt and Business Debt

Past due zakāt is deductible, for it is also considered as debt.[37]

Business debt should not be deducted from personal assets. It should be taken into consideration when calculating income from business.

Duplication of Zakāt is Prohibited

Once zakāt is paid on an asset, it does not accrue zakāt again until one full lunar year passes from the date when zakāt became due, for the *sharīʿa* does not allow duplication of zakāt. For example, if one pays zakāt on his livestock and then sells the remaining livestock, then there is no zakāt due on the money received from the sale during that zakāt year even if that money remains as savings. Similarly, when one pays zakāt on a salary, then zakāt is not due on the savings resulting from that salary, or asset purchased by that salary (such as shares), until it has been kept for one year.

Earned Income

Regarding zakāt on earned income, al-Qaraḍāwī writes, *"In view of the texts on zakāt, its objectives, and the general interests of Islam and Muslims, I believe that zakāt is due on earned income, whether salaries, wages, professional fees, or return on capital invested in other trade, such as shipping, planes, and hotels, when received, without the requirement of the passage of one year."*[38] He dedicates a full chapter called "Zakāt on Earnings" on this issue where he provides convincing arguments in support of this opinion.

Zakāt on earned income strongly resembles zakāt on agricultural output.[39] In our time, professional people earn much more income than village farmers. It would be contrary to justice that the *sharīʿa* would exempt the former from zakāt while requiring the latter to pay it. Earned income is also one of the most common sources of income in modern times. Exempting this from zakāt would deprive the poor of their due share in the wealth of the rich.

Subjecting earned income to zakāt is not without precedence in the classic texts. Among the Companions, Ibn ʿAbbās, Ibn Masʿūd, and Muʿāwiya considered earned income to be zakātable. From subsequent jurists, ʿUmar ibn ʿAbdul-ʿAzīz, al-Ḥasan, az-Zuhrī, and al-Awzāʿī supported this view.[40] It is reported that ʿUmar ibn ʿAbdul-ʿAzīz used to deduct the due zakāt from the salary of the soldiers.[41]

Among modern scholars who consider earned income to be zakātable are ʿAbdur-Rahmān Ḥasan, Muḥammad Abū Zahra, ʿAbdul-Wahhāb Khallāf, Shaykh Muḥammad al-Ghazālī, Monzer Kahf, and Abū Saʿūd.[42] Al-Ghazālī says, *"The conclusion is that whoever has an income equal to that of zakāt-paying farmers must be subject to zakāt on an equal footing regardless of capital and related conditions. Consequently, physicians, lawyers, and other professionals and employees are subject to zakāt on their income ..."*.[43]

According to the above contemporary jurists, the passage of one year is not necessary on earned income. There is no authentic *ḥadīth* about requiring passage of one year on earnings, al-Qaraḍāwī argues. Like agricultural produce, the income becomes zakātable when it is earned.[44] (See also *Net Earnings vs. Gross Earnings* and *Tax Returns*.)

While this has been the position adopted by this book, it should be mentioned that many classic jurists including Imāms Abū Ḥanīfa, Mālik, and ash-Shāfiʿī consider the passage of one year as required before zakāt is due on earned income. However, according to Imām Abū Ḥanīfa, if the owner has similar assets which, when added with the earned income, reaches *niṣāb* then zakāt is due at that time.

Interest Income

See *Shares and Bonds* on page 53.

Jewelry and Ornaments

According to Imām Aḥmad and Imām Shāfiʿī, there is no zakāt on women's jewelry and ornaments. This is also the opinion of al-Qaraḍāwī who considers jewelry, whether made of gold, silver, pearls or precious stones, to be exempt from zakāt if they are within the customary limit. If they reach extravagance or are used to hoard wealth, then the extra becomes subject to zakāt.[45]

F.S.A. Majeed says in his *Islamic Law* series that there is no zakāt on diamonds and other precious stones.[46] This opinion, in our view, is not in accordance with the spirit of the *sharīʿa* which subjects the wealth of the rich to zakāt.

Some precious stones, such as diamonds, are much more valuable than gold-made jewelry and can be used to hoard wealth. These items should, therefore, be considered within the category of jewelry.

Niṣāb on jewelry is 85 grams of gold and the zakāt rate is 2.5%.

Livestock

Livestock animals are zakātable. However, animals for personal use such as eating, riding, or transportation are exempt from zakāt.[47] Also exempt are working animals that are used for cultivation, carrying water, etc. The animals must be kept for at least one year before zakāt is due on them. The animals given as zakāt should be free of defects, illness, and old age and it should be of average type, not the best or the worst kind.[48]

Niṣāb and rate of zakāt on various animals are as follows:

Number of Animals	Zakāt Due
0–4 camels	None
5–9 camels	1 sheep
10–14 camels	2 sheep
15–19 camels	3 sheep
0–29 cows	None
30–39 cows	1 one-year-old cow
40–59 cows	1 two-year-old cow
60–69 cows	2 one-year-old cows
1–39 sheep	None
40–120 sheep	1 sheep
121–200 sheep	2 sheep
201–300 sheep	3 sheep[49]

Loans Made to Others

According to the majority of scholars, if the loan (i.e., receivable amount from others) is expected to be paid back then it should be considered part of the current assets and zakāt should be paid on it. If the loan is not expected to be paid back then it is not subject to zakāt, according to al-Qaraḍāwī and Imām Abū Ḥanīfa. If the money is ever paid, then it should be treated like a newly acquired asset on which zakāt would be due after a year has passed.[50]

Loss of Zakāt before it is Disbursed

See *If One Dies Before Paying Zakāt* on page 11.

Lost Property

There is no zakāt on lost property. If it is regained then it starts a new zakāt year. In other words, no zakāt is due for the period when it was lost. Lost property is treated in the same way as bad debts.[51]

Merchandise and Inventoried Items

All four schools of thought including contemporary scholars such as al-Qaraḍāwī, Sābiq, and Mawdūdī agree that zakāt is compulsory on merchandise and trading goods.[52] If a lunar year passes and the merchandise or the trading goods reach *niṣāb*, which is the value of 85g of gold, zakāt becomes due. Merchandise and trading goods include any items or properties that are intended for resale. Thus they include foodstuff, clothing, gift items, cars, parts, real estate properties, and the like. Scholars base their arguments on various texts. Here we reproduce the following relevant reports:

> Samura ibn Jundub said that "The Prophet (peace be upon him) used to order us to pay zakāt on what we had for sale."[53]

> Abū ʿAmr reported from his father that he said: I used to sell leather and containers. Once ʿUmar ibn al-Khaṭṭāb passed by me and said, "Pay the *ṣadaqa* due on your property." I said, "O Commander of the Faithful, it is just leather." He replied, "Evaluate it and then pay its due *ṣadaqa*."[54]

> Abū ʿUbayd reports from Ibn ʿUmar, "Slaves and clothes intended for sale are subject to zakāt."[55]

It is unfortunate that despite this unanimous agreement among the major jurists about the obligation of zakāt on merchandise and trading goods, many business and retail store owners are not serious about paying zakāt on them. This is nothing short of violating one of the obligatory pillars of Islam and the rights of the poor. Indeed, merchants are encouraged to pay more charity beyond the obligatory zakāt considering the fact that "*merchants need purification more than anyone else, because the way they earn their wealth may not always be clean*."[56] The Prophet (peace be upon him) said:

> O merchants, sales are associated with vain talk and swearing, so let it be mixed with *ṣadaqa*.[57]

In another *ḥadīth*, the Prophet (peace be upon him) said:

> Merchants are resurrected wicked on the Day of Judgment, except for those who fear Allah, speak the truth and are righteous.[58]

These warnings certainly are not for those merchants and businessmen who "fear Allah, speak the truth and are righteous", and the Prophet (peace be upon him) himself was a merchant at one time. Righteous merchants with their added leverage of financial resources can support many good services for the community that ordinary salaried people are not able to despite having good intentions. Such righteousness, however, requires paying the due zakāt and obeying the commandments of Allah (swt).

Anyone who has doubts about the zakātability on merchandise may learn more about this in *fiqh* books, such as *Fiqh us-Sunna* or *Fiqh uz-Zakāt*. (For more discussion about this topic and how to calculate zakāt, see *Business Goods and Business Income* on page 27.)

Minimum Standard of Living

The *sharīʿa* considers those assets as non-existent that are needed to fulfill basic needs. *Niṣāb*, therefore, is calculated from assets that are in excess of the basic needs, such as food, shelter, clothes, household utensils, furniture, money to pay back debts, basic transportation, books of knowledge, etc. for the zakāt payer, his household, and other family members he is required to support under the *sharīʿa*.[59]

Can we determine an amount that can be used by all zakāt payers as the standard deduction? Al-Qaraḍāwī says in this regard, *"... the essential needs of human beings evolve and change with time and circumstances, so determining them should be left to people of intelligence and understanding and to the exertion of best effort* (ijtihād) *of the proper authorities in the Islamic state."*[60]

When an Islamic state does not exist or when the standard deduction amount is not decided upon by the scholars of a given country, then our opinion is that the individual zakāt payer should calculate the deduction amount to the best of his sincerity. It should, however, be kept in mind that the deduction should include only the basic necessities. Al-Qaraḍāwī says, *"We should, however, note that this condition refers to essential or basic needs. People have an infinite amount of needs, especially in this time of ours, when many goods that used to be considered luxuries have become necessities. Not anything that is desired can be considered a basic need, since if the son of Adam had two valleys full of gold, he would want to obtain a third one. Basic needs are those human beings cannot survive without, such as food, shelter, clothing, and items needed for a job, such as books for study and tools for work."*[61] (See also *Niṣāb*.)

Net Earnings vs. Gross Earnings

"Zakāt on earned income applies only to the net amount", is the opinion of al-Qaraḍāwī. He also says while discussing zakāt on buildings, *"zakāt must be calculated on the basis of net income, after deducting expenses and costs such as wages, maintenance, taxes, debts, etc."* A minimum standard of living should also be deducted, unless it is already deducted from other assets. The remaining is zakātable if it reaches *niṣāb*, or when combined with other zakātable money, reaches *niṣāb*.[62]

Following this opinion, we may conclude that zakāt should apply only on net or "take home" salary or wage after income taxes and other deductibles (except voluntary deductions, such as pension contribution) are taken out. This is also the view of Kahf who says that salaries, business profits and professional earnings are subject to zakāt *"after deducting state and federal taxes, F.I.C.A., other taxes and a minimum level of living allowances."*[63]

According to Abū Saʿūd, the gross salary before taxes are deducted should be subject to zakāt. The argument he provides in support of this view is that zakāt should be imposed before taxes are imposed, since duties to Allah (swt) should come before duties to human beings, and therefore zakāt should be paid first before paying taxes. The second argument is that by paying taxes the zakāt payer receives benefit from the government in terms of the services it provides to the citizens. This is analogous to one buying amenities. Therefore, zakāt should be imposed on the gross amount before these amenities are purchased.[64]

This opinion, we believe, would contradict the care and consideration that *sharīʿa* gives to the zakāt payer, such as by deducting debts, expenses and essential needs and by using *niṣāb*, before making his assets liable to zakāt. If taxes were a voluntary contribution and one could decide whether to pay tax or not, then it would have been justified to impose zakāt on the gross income. But taxes are not voluntary contributions. An individual has no choice but to pay it. As a matter of fact taxes are already taken out from the gross wage before one receives his wage. Many modern states levy a high amount of taxes on earnings, from 15% to as much as 40% or more. How can zakāt be imposed on an amount that one never received or never had control of? The second argument also does not merit, for an individual is not responsible for circumstances that are beyond his control. If a government imposes taxes before zakāt is calculated, then an individual's intention cannot be questioned. In our opinion, it would clearly be an injustice to the zakāt payer to subject him to pay both tax and zakāt on his gross wage without deducting one from the other.

Imposing zakāt on net earnings is also consistent with the general principle that zakāt is payable only on assets that remain after all associated expenses, minimum standard of living, and debts are subtracted from them so that the zakāt payer is not put to unbearable hardship.

If the contribution is voluntary, as is the case with a pension contribution, then our opinion is that it should be zakātable unless it is considered a basic need, such as a deduction for medical insurance.[65] (See also *Earned Income* and *Tax Returns*.)

Niṣāb

Zakāt is not imposed unless the zakātable wealth reaches a certain minimum level. That level is called the *niṣāb*. For example, if one has 4 camels then there is no zakāt on the camels, but if he has at least 5 camels, then zakāt is due on his camels. *Niṣāb* on camels, therefore, is 5 camels.

Different types of assets have different *niṣābs*. For example, *niṣāb* on money is 85 grams of gold, *niṣāb* on camels is 5 camels, and *niṣāb* on grain is 653 kilograms. Zakāt on each type of asset is calculated separately. If one has 4 camels and 85 grams or more of gold or an equivalent amount of money, then he does not pay any zakāt on the camels he owns but pays zakāt on the gold or money.

Niṣāb must be in excess of the basic needs of the owner. Assets used to satisfy basic necessities are considered non-existent from the point of view of zakāt. Basic needs are food, shelter, clothes, household utensils, furniture, money to pay back debts, basic transportation, books of knowledge, etc.[66] To clarify this, let us assume that *niṣāb* on money is $1,000 and a family of four needs $20,000 per year to fulfill its basic needs in a particular locality. If the head of that family earns $20,500 in the zakāt year and he does not have any other monetary wealth, then from the viewpoint of zakāt he has only $500. This is short of the $1,000 *niṣāb* on money and, consequently, there is no zakāt on his money. However, if in addition to his income he also has cash savings of $800 from the previous year, then his wealth from the viewpoint of zakāt is $1,300 ($500 + $800). This is at or above *niṣāb* on money, and therefore zakāt is due on $1,300.

Niṣāb should not be confused with the amount required for a minimum standard of living. *Niṣāb* is a well-defined term in the *sharīʿa* that means a specific amount or quantity for a specific type of wealth for the purpose of calculating zakāt.

Combining Different Types of Assets

Can different types of assets be added together and zakāt imposed if the total value reaches *niṣāb*? This, in our view, is not supported by the *sharīʿa*. During the time of the Prophet (peace be upon him), zakāt was imposed on a particular type of asset only if that asset reached or exceeded *niṣāb* without it being added to other types of assets. There is no precedence of adding the value of different types of assets together, such as gold, agricultural produce, livestock, honey, etc. and paying zakāt on the total value if that reaches or exceeds *niṣāb*. Regarding combining assets Sābiq says:

> If a person owns gold and silver, but neither of them on its own constitutes a *niṣāb*, he should not combine the two in order to obtain a *niṣāb*. This is because they are not the same kind. The basic rule is that no category can be combined with another.[67]

However, the same type of wealth having the same *niṣāb* may be added together and zakātability can be assessed on the total. For example, all sources of money can be added together, such as wages and salaries, business income, savings, etc., and zakāt paid if the total reaches *niṣāb*. (See also *Minimum Standard of Living*.)

Passage of One Year

Passage of one lunar year is required before zakāt can be imposed on certain assets. There are two kinds of assets for the purpose of calculating zakāt: earned assets and non-earned assets. Earned assets, according to some contemporary jurists, do not require passage of a year.[68] These include wages and salaries, business income, rent income, etc. They also include crops, fruits, honey, extracted mineral, treasure, etc. These are zakātable when the earning occurs. Non-earned assets require passage of a year for zakāt to be imposed. These assets include livestock, trading goods (anything that is obtained for the purpose of resale), and money (savings). Out of these assets, only those are zakātable that have been kept for at least one lunar year.[69]

Property for Personal and Family Use

Property that is held for personal and family use is not subject to zakāt. Therefore, there is no zakāt on a residential house used by the family, clothing, utensils, tools, books, etc.[70]

Property on Public Trust

Property on public trust, such as property designated for the mosque, the poor, school, hospital, orphans, etc. are not subject to zakāt.[71]

Public Corporations

Either corporations should pay zakāt on net profit or individual shareholders should pay zakāt on the value of shares and earnings, but not both since that will result in duplication of zakāt. It should be left with the zakāt administration, when that exists, to decide which method to use.[72] In our form, we choose individual shareholders to be the zakāt payers. (See also *Shares and Bonds.*)

Rent

Zakāt on rented property is similar to that of business that uses exploited assets (not trading goods). Zakāt is calculated on the net rent income after deducting all expenses, such as loan payments, cost of repairs, insurance, property tax, and estimated income tax.

Zakāt is assessed on rent based on the principle that when fixed assets are used to generate growth, zakāt is assessed on the growth only and the fixed asset itself is exempted from zakāt. On the growth, zakāt is assessed at the rate of 10% of the net income or 5% of the gross income. This is consistent with the laws of zakāt on crops where zakāt is not assessed on agricultural land but on the growth of the land (i.e., the crop) at the rate of 10% on the net produce (i.e., watered by rain, and thus the expenses are covered for) or 5% of the gross produce. Based on that principle, buildings are exempted from zakāt but their growth (i.e., rent) is subjected to zakāt at the rate of 10% of the net income.

For rental business that rents equipment, cars, etc., zakāt is imposed on the value of the rental equipment (which are considered as trading goods) and the net income of the business. See *Business* on page 27 for further discussion.

Retirement Fund (401k Fund)

Typically, pension funds (specifically 401k funds in the US), are managed as follows: an employee makes optional contributions to his pension fund. The contributions are deducted from his salary cheques and are done pre-tax, meaning no tax is deducted from the money contributed to the 401k fund. Employers usually also contribute to the employee's 401k fund by matching a certain percentage of the contribution made by the employee. This fund grows – by contribution and investment – and is returned to the employee when he reaches retirement age. At that time, taxes are charged on the fund and the employee receives what is left after paying taxes. Until the time of retirement, the fund is managed by an independent agency. The employee cannot use the fund or any part of it at will, since the fund is not supposed to be withdrawn until the time of retirement. If the employee must withdraw the money, then that requires certain procedures to be followed first. And when the money is withdrawn, both tax and penalty are imposed on the amount taken and the employee receives the remaining amount.

According to al-Qaraḍāwī, if the contributor has access to the fund and can spend it at will, then zakāt is due every year on the fund like someone who pays zakāt on loans made to others that are expected to be paid back. However, if he has no access to the fund then zakāt is to be given only when the money is received, that is at the time of retirement.[73]

The question that now arises is: should the 401k fund be considered a fund over which the employee does not have any control, or should it be considered a fund that is within the control of the employee? One who supports the former (no control) may argue that the fund is under the control of an independent agency and it is supposed to be kept as such until the time of retirement. If the employee wants to withdraw the fund, it can only be done after completing a formal procedure and paying a monetary penalty. Therefore, the fund should be considered as being beyond someone's disposal. For, obviously, he cannot spend from it at will. On the other hand, one may say that the fund *can* be considered under one's control since the employee has the right to withdraw the fund, though maybe with penalty.

In our opinion, the former opinion appears to be more acceptable since the 401k fund is beyond the direct control of the employee. For, it is managed by an independent agency and it is supposed to remain there until it reaches maturity at the time of retirement. Unlike savings in a bank account, an employee cannot use this money or any part of it at will. It is true that it can be considered like a good loan since it is also expected to be paid back. However, unlike a good loan the 401k fund will be returned to the employee only at the time of retirement, which can be many years in the future depending on the age of the employee. If he is required to pay zakāt on it every year, then he would likely be paying zakāt on a fund for many years although the fund was never available to him for his use.

If the 401k contributions are deducted from the salary cheque, then the deduction should be considered, in our opinion, as part of the net income and zakāt should be paid on it. For example, if one's gross salary cheque is for $5,000 and he receives a net cheque of $3,500 after the employer deducts $1,000 in income tax and $500 in 401k contribution, then his net income should be considered as $4,000 ($3,500 + $500) for the purpose of calculating zakāt on earnings. This is because unlike tax which the employee is required to pay, 401k contributions are optional. An employee always has the option not to contribute to the fund. (See also *Net Earnings vs. Gross Earnings.*)

Savings

Savings are subject to zakāt, which includes cash in hand, in bank accounts, and any uninvested cash that is kept with a stockbroker for investment. However, two things should be kept in mind when calculating zakāt on savings: (1) Only that portion of the savings is subject to zakāt that has been kept for one lunar year, and (2) Duplication of zakāt must be avoided. For example, if part of the savings comes from income on which the payer has already paid or calculated zakāt during that year, then that part should be deducted from the savings, for, otherwise, this will result in duplication of zakāt on the same asset during the same year.

It appears that the only way to correctly calculate zakāt on savings while satisfying the above two principles is to assess zakāt on the savings that the zakāt payer had prior to the beginning of the zakāt year, provided that the savings were maintained throughout the year. If at the end of the zakāt year the savings were reduced from what they were prior to the beginning of the zakāt year, then that lesser amount would be subject to zakāt.

To illustrate this, let us say that someone is calculating zakāt for the year of Ramaḍān 11, 1421 to Ramaḍān 10, 1422. Prior to the beginning of the zakāt year, which is Ramaḍān 10, 1421, he had total savings of $10,000 (current account, savings account, cash in hand, etc.). During the zakāt year, he earned $40,000, and at the end of the zakāt year, which is Ramaḍān 10, 1422, he had savings of $12,000. In that case, he will pay zakāt on $10,000 since he kept those savings for one year. If on Ramaḍān 10, 1422 his savings were $8,000, then he will pay zakāt on $8,000 since that is the amount he maintained for one year although he began with $10,000 savings prior to the beginning of the zakāt year.

The above example illustrates zakāt on savings only. The $40,000 earned income will also be subject to zakāt, which is discussed separately.

Shares and Bonds

Regarding zakāt on shares and bonds, al-Qaraḍāwī considers the opinions of Professors Abū Zahra, ʿAbdur Raḥmān Ḥasan, and Khallāf more suitable for individual zakāt payers. According to this opinion, shares and bonds are like trading goods. Zakāt, therefore, is 2.5% of the value of shares and bonds plus the returns (dividends) on them. Any associated expenses should be deducted before calculating the zakāt.[74] In our view, if any portion of the dividend earned is re-invested into purchasing more stocks, then that portion should be excluded from the earnings to avoid duplication of zakāt (since the value of the stock has already been subjected to zakāt). Also, the value of the stock should not include any uninvested cash that is kept with the broker. Such cash should be considered as part of the savings.

If shares and bonds are considered similar to trading goods, then it appears, in our opinion, that like trading goods only those shares and bonds should be subjected to zakāt that have been kept for one lunar year. Not doing so will likely result in duplication of zakāt since one can buy new shares using his earned income that has already been subjected to zakāt in the current year. A difficulty may arise in assessing zakātable shares for regular stock traders who are always buying and selling shares without keeping them for any length of time. In that case, our opinion is that the value of the shares prior to the beginning of the zakāt year and at the end of the zakāt year should be determined, and the lesser of the two should be considered the value of the shares that have been kept for one year.

According to the majority of scholars, the value of shares and bonds should be determined based on their price as of the due date of zakāt. Also, the wholesale price should be used, not the retail price.[75] For more discussion about assessing the value of shares, see *Determining the Value of a Given Asset* on page 30.

Interest Income

It should be noted here that bonds earn interest, which is prohibited in Islam. Regardless of the lawfulness of holding bonds, it is capital owned by people and zakāt on it should be discussed.[76] Our opinion is that no zakāt should be calculated on interest income. Instead, all interest income should be given away to the poor without expecting any reward in return since zakāt is due only on lawful money and one never becomes the lawful owner of prohibited assets. This is also the view of Kahf, who says:

> ... certain forms of wealth such as bonds, securities and savings accounts are included [in zakāt calculation] ... in spite of the prohibition of interest in Islam because Muslims own such assets. In all cases, where an asset of a Muslim is put to an unlawful use, only the principal amount will be considered for zakāt and not the interest accrued on it because interest does not become a property of Muslims.[77]

It is surprising that Abū-Sa'ūd considers interest income to be zakātable. Consequently, he provides a line for "Interest on bonds, loans, deposits, etc." in his zakāt form and adds this income to the zakāt payer's other assets and charges a 2.5% zakāt on the total.[78] He also says that "*any wealth (māl) possessed by a person ... must pay zakāt, even if the title of possession is illegal. Thus usurped or stolen wealth is not exempt from zakāt.*"[79] This, in our view, is contrary to the fundamental principle of *sharī'a* that one must have absolute ownership of the property on which zakāt is to be given, and one never becomes the owner of unlawful wealth. Such wealth must be returned to the original owners or, when that is impossible, given away to the poor in its entirety (see *Unlawful Wealth* on page 56 below). (See also *Public Corporations.*)

Tax

See *Net Earnings vs. Gross Earnings* for discussion about whether earned income should be subject to zakāt prior to or after subtracting taxes.

Tax Returns

Our opinion is that net earned income should be adjusted by the estimated tax refund or tax due when calculating zakāt on wages and salaries. In other words, the estimated tax refund should be added to the net income (since tax payments are deducted from income when calculating zakāt) and the estimated tax due should be deducted from the net income.

It is likely that tax refunds or additional tax payments will occur after zakāt has been calculated. Besides, the tax year cannot coincide with the zakāt year, which is lunar based. It is for this reason that the zakāt payer should use an estimated tax refund or estimated tax payment when calculating net earnings from wages and salaries. It is recommended that one use an estimate that might result in a higher net income than a lower one in order to avoid underassessment of zakāt. (See also *Earned Income, Net Earnings vs. Gross Earnings.*)

Unlawful Wealth

Zakāt is imposed on assets that are lawfully owned. Zakāt cannot be calculated on prohibited or unlawful wealth, such as interest income, stolen property, or wealth acquired or earned through unlawful means. Such wealth must be returned in full to its lawful owners.[80]

One cannot transform his unlawful wealth into lawful wealth by paying zakāt on it, nor does one get any reward by giving it away to the poor in its entirety. The Prophet (peace be upon him) said:

> He who acquires wealth by forbidden means, then gives it away as *ṣadaqa* gets no reward; the sins remain on him.[81]

In another *ḥadīth* he said:

> By Him in Whose Hand is my soul, no servant earns wealth unlawfully and gives it as *Ṣadaqa* but that it is not accepted from him, or spends it but that it is not blessed, or leaves it behind his back [after he dies] but that it is his means to the Fire. Allah does not erase evil with evil. He rather removes evil with good. A corrupt deed does not clear another corrupt deed.[82]

Wages and Salaries

See *Earned Income* on page 37.

Notes

23. *Fiqh uz-Zakāt*, pp. 228-229, 242.
24. *ibid.*, pp. 232, 239-240.
25. *ibid.*, pp. 255-256.
26. *ibid.*, pp. 203, 213-216.
27. *ibid.*, pp. 291, 296, 301-306.

28. *ibid.*, p. 256.

29. *ibid.*, p. 307.

30. *ibid.*, p. 42.

31. *ibid.*, p. 57.

32. *ibid.*, p. 218.

33. *ibid.*, pp. 90-94.

34. Sayyid Abu'l A'lā Mawdūdī, *Towards Understanding the Qur'ān*, The Islamic Foundation, Leicester, 1990, Vol. III, p. 224.

35. It should be stressed here that non-deductibility of debts on luxurious items is an opinion of the present author. Jurists who exempt debts from zakāt liability do not discuss whether the debt occurred due to purchase of a luxurious good.

36. This discussion should not be interpreted as an approval of obtaining interest-bearing loans. The objective here is only to discuss zakāt-exempt debt when one receives such loans.

37. *Fiqh uz-Zakāt*, p. 95.

38. *ibid.*, p. 321.

39. Zakāt is imposed on agricultural output – if it reaches *niṣāb* – without requiring the passage of a year.

40. *ibid.*, p. 311.

41. *Contemporary Zakāt*, p. 153.

42. Monzer Kahf, *The Calculation of Zakah*, The Muslim Students Association, Indiana, 1976, p. 5; Maḥmūd Abū-Sa'ūd, *About the Fiqh of Zakāt*, Zakāt and Research Foundation, Cincinnati, 1986, p. 20.

43. *Fiqh uz-Zakāt*, pp. 310, 325.

44. *ibid.*, pp. 313, 316, 321-322.

45. *ibid.*, pp. 184, 186-188, 192, 199.

46. F.S.A. Majeed, *Islamic Law, Vol II: Zakāt*, Ze Majeed's Publishing, Singapore, 1995, p. 67.

47. *Fiqh uz-Zakāt*, pp. 103-104.

48. *ibid.*, pp. 134, 137.

49. *ibid.*, pp. 106, 121, 131.

50. *ibid.*, pp. 74-76.

51. *ibid.*, p. 80.

52. *Fiqh us-Sunna*, pp. 18-20; *Fiqh uz-Zakāt*, pp. 203-208; Sayyid Abu'l A'lā Mawdūdī, *Let Us Be Muslims*, The Islamic Foundation, Leicester, 2000, p. 233.

53. Reported by Abū Dāwūd.

54. Reported by Ash-Shāfiʿī, Aḥmad, Abū ʿUbaid, ad-Dāraquṭnī, and al-Baihaqī.

55. *Al-Mughnī,* Vol. 3, p. 35. Cited by al-Qaraḍāwī, p. 207.

56. *Fiqh uz-Zakāt*, p. 209.

57. Reported by Abū Dāwūd. This should not be interpreted as an approval for unlawful dealings in business so long as one pays charity. Both the Qur'ān and the *Sunna* strictly prohibit cheating in business, which is also a violation of *ḥuqūq al-ʿibād.* Such acts are not forgiven unless the party who has been wronged forgives.

58. Reported by al-Tirmidhī.

59. *Fiqh uz-Zakāt*, pp. 86-88, 177, 308-309.

60. *ibid.*, p. 88.

61. *ibid.*, p. 87.

62. *ibid.*, pp. 329, 308.

63. *The Calculation of Zakah*, p. 5.

64. *About the Fiqh of Zakāt*, p. 38.

65. It needs to be stated here that the Western form of insurance is not considered Islamically lawful according to some scholars, including al-Qaraḍāwī. Therefore, whether medical insurance premiums are deductible can be debated.

66. *Fiqh uz-Zakāt,* pp. 86-87, 177.

67. *Fiqh us-Sunna*, p. 14.

68. Many classic jurists consider the passage of one year as necessary. See *Earned Income* for more discussion on this.

69. *Fiqh uz-Zakāt*, pp. 95-96.

70. *ibid.*, pp. 67, 79.

71. *ibid.*, p. 72.

72. *ibid.*, p. 338.

73. *ibid.*, p. 76.

74. *ibid.*, p. 335.

75. *ibid.*, p. 218.

76. *ibid.*, p. 331.

77. *The Calculation of Zakah*, p. 3.

78. *About the Fiqh of Zakāt*, p. 42.

79. *ibid.*, p. 13.

80. *Fiqh uz-Zakāt*, p. 72.

81. Reported by Ibn Khuzayma, Ibn Ḥibbān and al-Ḥākim. Cited by al-Qaraḍāwī, p. 544.

82. Reported by Aḥmad. Cited by al-Qaraḍāwī, p. 544.

CHAPTER ❖ 4

Disbursing Zakāt

Categories Where Zakāt Money Can be Spent

Allah (swt) says in the Qur'ān regarding distribution of zakāt:

> Zakāt is for the poor and the needy and those who are in charge thereof, those whose hearts are to be reconciled; and to free those in bondage, and to help those burdened with debt, and for expenditure in the way of Allah, and for the wayfarer. This is an obligation from Allah. Allah is All-Knowing, All-Wise. (9:60)

According to this verse, zakāt can be spent in the following eight categories:

The "Poor" and the "Needy" (*fuqarā'* and *masākīn*)

According to some scholars, these are two different categories where "poor" (*fuqarā'*) refers to a person who cannot make both ends meet but yet does not ask for help due to modesty and self-respect, while "needy" (*masākīn*) refers to those who are totally destitute.

According to most scholars, the people who are considered "poor" and "needy" and thus qualify to receive zakāt are those who have no property or income or those whose property or income falls short of satisfying the essential needs. According to Mawdūdī, this category includes those who are needy due to physical disability, old age, or accidental circumstances and also those who may become self-supporting again after receiving help.[83]

Those who are poor but do not reveal their desperate needs or ask for help due to their modesty qualify more to receive zakāt than those who beg.[84]

Full-time students who are in need of assistance to continue their education, regardless of whether the education is religious or secular, qualify to receive zakāt according to al-Qaraḍāwī.[85]

Workers in Zakāt Administration (*ʿāmīlna ʿalayhā*)

Those who collect and distribute zakāt can receive zakāt according to verse 9:60. This indicates, according to al-Qaraḍāwī, that *"zakāt collection and administration is the function of an organized body of paid employees."* These workers can receive compensation regardless of whether they are poor or not and the compensation should be competitive with the market value of their labour.[86]

Those Whose Hearts are Being Reconciled (*mu'allafatu'l qulūb*)

This includes people who recently became Muslim, those whose evil acts can be prevented, and those who need to strengthen their commitment to the faith. According to some jurists including the Ḥanafīs and the Mālikīs, this category is no longer available after the death of the Prophet (peace be upon him) since Islam by then was made victorious. Al-Qaraḍāwī's opinion is that the need for funding in this category has not ceased. However, the decision to spend money in this category and whom to pay can only be made by the Islamic state, not individual zakāt payers.[87]

That this category has not ceased to exist is also the view of Mawdūdī. According to him, Muslim converts, even if they are wealthy, *"may be given zakāt to reconcile them by showing at first hand the caring nature of Islam"*.[88]

Emancipating Slaves (*fi'r-riqāb*)

Zakāt money can be used to purchase a slave from his master in order to set him free.

"Islam was the first system", says al-Qaraḍāwī, *"to begin the gradual abolition of slavery through a combination of means."* One of the means among these is to spend zakāt money to emancipate slaves.[89] *"Under Islam"*, writes Quṭb, *"slaves became entitled to their freedom as soon as they demanded it, and they were helped to regain their liberty and dignity by allocating them money from charity and zakāt. Slaves would then become wage earners, entitled to receive zakāt. Every effort would be made to speed up their total freedom."*[90]

Those in Debt for Personal Reasons (*al-ghārimīn*)

People who are overwhelmed with debt and do not have enough income or assets to pay off the debt qualify to receive zakāt. The debt can be as a result of buying a house for family use, medical expenses, marriage, or consumer expenditure. Certain conditions, however, apply, such as:

1. The debtor must be in need of financial help.
2. The debt should be as a result of lawful activity, such as borrowing to support a family.
3. The debt should be due immediately, and
4. The debt should be to other individuals. Obligations to Allah (swt), such as past due zakāt or *kaffāra* are excluded.[91]

Islam takes a noble attitude towards people burdened with debt. "*Under Islam*", observes Quṭb, "*a debtor is never put under duress by either the creditor or the law, but is always given another chance to settle his debt. Furthermore, society at large will not stand idly by when a borrower is suffering genuine hardship because of his indebtedness. ... insolvent debtors who borrow money for legitimate purposes and are unable to pay it back, qualify for help from zakāt funds to help them clear such liabilities and alleviate their situation, provided that their debts were incurred for legitimate purposes.*"[92]

How compassionate Islam is towards the members of the society! What a noble attitude Islam wants them to foster in their hearts towards one another! Al-Qaraḍāwī remarks:

> Islam teaches Muslims moderation and economy in living and encourages them to avoid borrowing. If circumstances force Muslims to borrow, they must do so after careful planning and with the full intention of paying back the loan. ... If a debtor is unable to pay some or all of his debts in spite of evidence that shows his good intentions, the state saves him from the burden and humiliation of debt. It is said that "debts are a source of depression in the night and humiliation in the day." ... Debts are not only a source of anxiety and insecurity for the

> borrower, they also affect the borrower's behaviour and morality. ... [By paying from the zakāt fund], Islam frees debtors from the obligation and humiliation of their debts. The world has never known another system which includes in its very constitution the rights of debtors to financial aid.[93]

Can the debt of deceased people be paid from zakāt? According to al-Qaraḍāwī, the texts of the *sharīʿa* do not prevent that possibility. Muhammad bin Jamil Zeno also considers this permissible.[94]

For the Cause of Allah (*fī sabīlillāh*)

The seventh category where zakāt can be spent according to verse 9:60 is spending "in the way of Allah". All four schools of thought agree that this refers to *jihād* or fighting for the sake of Allah. This is also the view of al-Qaraḍāwī, who argues that the verse cannot have a general meaning of spending for any Islamic cause since the verse lists specific categories where zakāt can be spent. He, however, considers other activities in this category as well that achieve the same goal as fighting,[95] such as:

1. Fighters of opposing ideologies, since *jihād* is not restricted to military action. Therefore, this category includes writing, lecturing, and organizing work to support or defend Islam.
2. Fighting in defence of a Muslim land provided that one fights not simply for the love of his country but for Islam.
3. Building Islamic schools, libraries, etc. are not considered as *jihād*. However, if these are desperately needed in a country dominated by

secularists and communists, then establishing such institutions can be considered for receiving zakāt in order to protect the Muslim children from destructive ideologies.

4. Organizing work to re-establish the Islamic state and Islamic society in the "political, cultural, and economic domains". According to al-Qaraḍāwī, *"cultural, educational and informational* jihād *in the Way of Allah should be given priority today as long as such* jihād *is a purely Islamic effort that aims at re-establishing the Islamic state."*
5. Building *da'wa* centres that provide correct information about Islam.
6. Establishing Islamic centres "to provide Islamic education and training and protect the faith of Muslim youth from deviation, agnosticism, and behavioural corruption."
7. Establishing Islamic newspapers or issuing Islamic books that provide guidance and increase political and social awareness among Muslims.
8. Providing full-time workers in the Way of Allah.

Travellers (*ibnus-sabīl*)

According to some contemporary scholars this category of people has ceased to exist due to modern communication systems and financial networks that facilitate transferring money from one place to another quickly. Al-Qaraḍāwī's opinion is that "travellers" are still available today who need assistance. Among the examples he provides are the following:

1. Some people do not do banking and they may be far away from their home and be in need of money.

2. Refugees who are driven away from their home by oppressors and dictators.
3. Those who want to initiate a journey for public service or affairs that are beneficial to the public.
4. Street beggars (according to some Ḥanafīs).
5. Foundling infants who have no homes (according to Rashīd Riḍā').

The condition for the traveller to receive zakāt is that the traveller must be in need of money when on the road. Also, the travelling should not be in disobedience to Allah but for a valid cause, such as *ḥajj, jihād*, seeking knowledge, searching for a job, or conducting business.[96]

Priority of Spending

Zakāt money should be spent in the above categories according to their priorities and based on actual needs and public interest. But it is important to keep in mind that **the primary recipient of zakāt is the poor and the needy**. Helping such people is the main objective of zakāt.[97]

Who Cannot Receive Zakāt

The Rich

This category also includes children of those who are rich and those whose living expenses are the responsibility of a wealthy person.

Those Capable of Earning

Anyone who chooses to live on charity and the financial help of others despite being capable of earning is not qualified to receive zakāt. This is the opinion of al-Qaraḍāwī, and Shāfiʿī and Ḥanbalī scholars. However, physical power is not sufficient to disqualify one from receiving zakāt, which should be done only when the following conditions are met: (1) Existence of available and lawful employment, (2) The employment is within the ability of the person, (3) The employment is suitable for the person according to his social status, and (4) The employment earns him sufficient money to fulfill the needs of his family.[98]

Full-time Devotees Who Expend No Effort to Earn a Living

Anyone who completely devotes himself to worshipping without expending any effort to earn a livelihood despite being able to do so does not qualify to receive zakāt.[99]

Can Non-Muslims Be Given Zakāt?

According to the majority of scholars, zakāt cannot be given to non-Muslims, atheists, and apostates. That is because zakāt is a religious tax which is charged only on the believers (non-Muslim citizens of an Islamic state are exempt from zakāt), and therefore it is to be distributed among the believers who are needy. In this respect, zakāt is comparable to the *tithe* that Mormons pay to their church. All scholars also agree that non-Muslims who fight against Islam or Muslims must not be given zakāt.[100]

Yet, al-Qaraḍāwī's opinion is that although the zakāt fund is primarily for Muslims, there is no textual evidence that forbids helping non-Muslims who are poor from the zakāt fund if that does not harm the poor Muslims who are the primary recipients of zakāt.[101]

This is regarding helping non-Muslims from the zakāt fund. But all poor and needy people regardless of their religious affiliation can always be helped from other funds, such as the charity fund if they do not fight against Islam or Muslims.[102] Many Qur'ānic verses and the *ḥadīths* of the Prophet (peace be upon him) instruct or encourage Muslims to help the needy without limiting that directive to Muslims only. Allah (swt) says:

> And they feed, for the love of Allah, the indigent, the orphan, and the captive (saying), "We feed you for the sake of Allah alone ..." (76:8-9)

> ... It is righteousness to believe in Allah and the Last Day and the Angels and the Book, and the Messengers; to spend of your substance, out of love for Him, for your kin, for orphans, for the needy, for the wayfarer, for those who ask, and for the ransom of slaves ... Such are the people of truth, the God-fearing. (2:177)

The Prophet (peace be upon him) once said to his wife ʿĀ'isha:

> Do not turn away a poor man, ʿĀ'isha, even if all you can give is half a date. If you love the poor and bring them near you, ʿĀ'isha, Allah will bring you near Him on the Day of Resurrection.[103]

Such is the noble attitude of Islam towards the members of humanity. It should also be mentioned here that Islam puts tremendous emphasis on Muslims to be good to their neighbours. Muslims are asked to be gentle and caring to their neighbours – be they Muslim or otherwise. They should always inquire about their well-being and forthwith come to their assistance whenever they are in need. This is their right that Islam grants them over their Muslim neighbours. The Prophet (peace be upon him) is reported to have said:

> A neighbour has more right to be taken care of by his neighbour (than by those who live afar).[104]

Close Relatives

According to Sābiq and other jurists, grandparents, parents, children, grandchildren, and wives of zakāt payers cannot be given zakāt since they consider the zakāt payer to be responsible for their expenses.[105] After examining the opinions of various jurists on this, al-Qaraḍāwī considers giving zakāt to all relatives as appropriate if they are needy except parents, children, and wives.[106]

As for giving zakāt to a poor husband by his rich wife, most jurists agree that it is permissible or even preferred. Abū Ḥanīfa differs on this although his two great disciples consider this allowable.[107] Both Sābiq and al-Qaraḍāwī argue in support of permissibility.[108] The following *ḥadīth* narrated by Zainab, the wife of Ibn Masʿūd, is usually quoted in support of this view. She came to the Prophet (peace be upon him) and said:

> O Prophet of Allah! Indeed you have ordered us today to give away *ṣadaqa*. But Ibn Masʿūd claims that he and his children deserve it more than someone else. The Prophet, upon whom be peace, responded, "Ibn Masʿūd is right. Your husband and your children are more deserving."[109]

It should be reminded, however, that the husband should be poor and needy enough to be considered a zakāt recipient.

Sinful People May Be Given Zakāt

The pious and righteous people who are needy and yet do not ask for help or disclose their needs due to modesty deserve assistance from the zakāt fund more than others. That does not, however, mean that other Muslims should not be helped. According to Mawdūdī, there is no basis in the Qur'ān or the *aḥadīths* for barring sinful people from receiving zakāt. He says:

> The broad principles of Islam also indicate that a person's sinfulness does not disqualify him from receiving help. Rendering assistance to sinful people in times of dire need, and a generally graceful and benevolent attitude towards them, often serves as an effective means of reforming them.[110]

Other Considerations

Intention

According to most jurists intention is required when paying zakāt, which need not be expressed in words. Intention is also needed so that payment of zakāt can be distinguished from other charitable donations.[111]

Payment in Value

Al-Qaraḍāwī agrees with the Ḥanafī view that zakāt does not have to be paid in kind but can also be paid in value.

For example, if one is required to pay zakāt on his crops, then he is permitted to pay the monetary value of the amount of crop that is to be given as zakāt.[112]

Area of Distribution

All scholars agree that zakāt should be distributed in the same area from where the zakāt is collected. Sābiq argues that this is "*because zakāh aims at freeing the poor inhabitants of an area from want, and thus its transfer would contribute to their deprivation.*"[113] One of the *aḥadīths* used in support of this view is the one narrated by Mu'ādh who was sent as a zakāt administrator by the Prophet (peace be upon him). The instruction given to him to be delivered to his people was:

> Tell them that there is a charity due upon them to be taken from their rich and to be given back to their poor.[114]

However, if deemed necessary then the state can spend some of the zakāt collected in other areas. That should be done after due consideration only. When zakāt is disbursed by individual zakāt payers themselves, then, according to al-Qaraḍāwī, "*individual payers can assume the same role [as the state] and decide whether to transport zakāt to needy relatives, to people who are in dire need, for essential interests of Muslims, or to a pivotal Islamic project in another country.*"[115]

Pre-Payment and Delayed Payment

Zakāt is due immediately; payment of zakāt, therefore, should not be delayed unless there is a reason to wait in order to give it to needy relatives or anyone else in need.[116]

Pre-payment is allowed according to most jurists on assets that require passage of one year, such as livestock, money, and trading goods if the payer has the necessary *niṣāb.*[117]

Informing the Recipient that it is Zakāt

Preferably, the recipient should not be told that what is being given is zakāt. There are people who would hesitate to receive zakāt due to their modesty, while there are others who are doubtful about whether they are qualified to receive zakāt. If the payer considers the recipient to be poor and deserving of zakāt, then that will suffice and no other verification will be needed.[118]

Prayer by the Recipient for the Zakāt Payer

Being grateful and appreciative is characteristic of all good-hearted people. This is more so for a believer who is ever grateful for all the bounties of life and property granted by Allah (swt) that he or she enjoys. Such a person never fails to appreciate any assistance, however small, rendered to him by others. In this modern time of ours when individualism and a self-centred life-style is becoming the norm, especially in the industrial world, coming forward and helping the needy is a sign of love, compassion, and sacrifice that contrasts sharply with that self-centric phenomenon. This is exactly what the zakāt payer does. He gives up part of his wealth for his fellow brethren who are in need. He receives no earthly benefit in return, nor does he expect any. In many cases, he is not even known or identified to those who are benefited by his zakāt. This sacrifice he does not just once or twice but continues year after year so long as he is blessed by Allah (swt) with a certain amount of wealth.

A zakāt receiver should, therefore, pray for blessings and mercy for those from whose zakāt he is benefited, even though he may not know their identity. It is narrated from ʿAbdullāh ibn Abū ʿAwfa that upon receiving zakāt (as zakāt administrator), the Prophet (peace be upon him) would say:

> O Allah, bless the family of Abū ʿAwfa.[119]

Once a man paid his zakāt with a camel. At this, the Prophet (peace be upon him) prayed:

> May Allah bless him and make his camels beneficial to him.[120]

Indeed, Allah (swt) Himself asked the zakāt receivers to pray for the zakāt payers:

> Take alms of their property that you may purify and sanctify them and pray for them. Verily, your prayers are a comfort for them. (9:103)

How Just and Equitable is Allah (swt)! While He enjoins zakāt on those who are wealthy, He asks the zakāt receivers to pray for them, and He exalts them, saying that their prayers are a comfort for the zakāt givers! This is truly a wonderful transaction that is conducted exactly according to the commandments of Allah (swt). What can, therefore, fall on these two parties other than a shower of blessings and *ḥasanāt* from Allah (swt) in this world and the Next?

Notes

83. *Towards Understanding the Qur'ān*, Vol. III, p. 221; *Let Us Be Muslims*, p. 234.

84. *Fiqh uz-Zakāt*, pp. 345, 348, 354.

85. *ibid.*, p. 353.

86. *ibid.*, pp. 366, 373.

87. *ibid.*, pp. 377, 381, 388.

88. *Towards Understanding the Qur'ān*, Vol. III, p. 223; *Let Us Be Muslims*, p. 235.

89. *Fiqh uz-Zakāt*, p. 394.

90. *In the Shade of the Qur'ān*, Vol. I, p. 173.

91. *Fiqh uz-Zakāt*, pp. 397-399.

92. *In the Shade of the Qur'ān*, Vol. I, p. 371.

93. *Fiqh uz-Zakāt*, pp. 399-400.

94. Muhammad bin Jamil Zeno, *The Pillars of Islam and Iman*, Dar-us-Salam Publications, Riyadh, 1996, p. 172.

95. *Fiqh uz-Zakāt*, pp. 421-428.

96. *ibid.*, pp. 434, 436-437.

97. *ibid.*, p. 443.

98. *ibid.*, pp. 350-352.

99. *ibid.*, p. 353.

100. *Fiqh us-Sunna*, p. 73.

101. *Fiqh uz-Zakāt*, p. 452.

102. *ibid.*, p. 448.

103. Reported by al-Tirmidhī, Bayhaqī and Ibn Māja.

104. Reported by Bukhārī.

105. *Fiqh us-Sunna*, p. 75.

106. *Fiqh uz-Zakāt*, p. 461.

107. This is not relevant here, but it is interesting to note that these two great disciples of Imām Abū Ḥanīfa – Imām Abū Yūsuf and Imām Muḥammad – differed with their teacher on this and other occasions. This shows their open-minded intellect as well as their independent judgment despite the overwhelming personality and unusual talent of their master in *fiqh, kalām,* law, commerce, and other disciplines. Indeed, he is still known as *Imām-i-A'ẓam* and the *Master of Analogy* and independent reasoning. Also interesting to note is that in certain matters, Abū Ḥanīfa retracted his own opinion and adopted the opinions of his two disciples who differed with him. This shows the humility and open-mindedness of the Imām himself despite the fact that he became famous and well-respected throughout the Muslim world during his own lifetime. Such was the character of the early imāms and scholars. It

is said that even if they differed on an issue they still showed great respect for the others who disagreed with them, and were ready to accept another opinion if that turned out to have better *dalīl* (evidence). Abū Ḥanīfa is reported to have said, "Ours is no more than an opinion. We do not oblige or coerce anyone into accepting it. Whoever has a better judgment, let him advance it." (See Ṭāhā Jābir al-ʿAlwānī, *Ethics of Disagreement in Islam*, IIIT, 1993, p. 60.) There is much to be learned from these great past luminaries. They left behind for us not only their life's work, but also the shining example of their conduct.

108. *Fiqh us-Sunna*, p. 79; *Fiqh uz-Zakāt*, p. 457.
109. Reported by al-Bukhārī, Aḥmad, and others.
110. *Towards Understanding the Qur'ān*, Vol. III, p. 225.
111. *Fiqh uz-Zakāt*, p. 503.
112. *ibid.*, p. 509.
113. *Fiqh us-Sunna*, p. 81.
114. Reported by al-Tirmidhī.
115. *Fiqh uz-Zakāt*, pp. 511, 517. *Let Us Be Muslims*, p. 237.
116. *Fiqh uz-Zakāt*, pp. 518, 522.
117. *ibid.*, p. 519.
118. *ibid.*, p. 531.
119. Reported by Aḥmad.
120. Reported by an-Nasā'ī.

CHAPTER ❖ 5

Zakāt Calculation

Preparations Before Using the Form

Gathering Necessary Information and Documents

How much time should I spend in calculating my zakāt? Calculation of zakāt should be taken as seriously, if not more seriously, as preparing a tax return, for it is not only an obligation towards the poor (or the zakāt administration) but also an obligatory act of worship of Allah (swt). The zakāt payer should not expect to calculate his or her zakāt in five or ten minutes but should be mentally prepared to spend a sufficient amount of time to calculate the zakāt as accurately as possible and to the best of his or her intention and sincerity.

The zakāt payer should collect the necessary documents and information before sitting down to calculate the zakāt. These preparations include:

- Collect bank statements that show your balance at the beginning and end of the zakāt year. Make reasonable estimates of your cash balance on hand. If you use software to manage your finances, you may easily find both your bank and cash balances in your financial software. Also, find the amount of any uninvested cash that is kept with your broker.

- Collect documents, such as cheque stubs about wages, salaries, pensions, and other earnings you received during the zakāt year.
- Make a list of your outstanding personal debts, when the debt occurred, and the payments which have been made so far towards those debts.
- Make a list of outstanding loans you made to others and when the loans were made.
- *If you have a business*, collect the necessary documents to help you calculate revenue, expenses, and net income of the business during the zakāt year.
- *If you have rental properties*, collect the necessary documents to calculate the rent amounts received and all associated expenses made during the zakāt year.
- *If you have shares and bonds*, make a list of all shares and bonds showing when they were purchased, their market value as of the zakāt end date, dividends received, and associated expenses.
- *If you have gold and jewelry items*, find their market value as of the zakāt end date. Note: Jewelry for personal use within a customary limit is exempted from zakāt.
- *If you have business and economic goods* that are intended for resale, make a list of them showing when they were purchased or obtained, and their estimated market value as of the zakāt end date.

- *If you have agricultural produce*, collect information about the total produce that occurred during the zakāt year and all associated expenses related to the farming of the produce.

This form does not calculate zakāt on livestock and other uncommon zakātable assets, such as mineral and buried treasure. Incorporating these assets into the form would add additional and undue complexities to the form, which would be burdensome for the vast majority of zakāt payers who do not have these types of assets. The principles of calculating zakāt on livestock have been discussed under *Livestock* on page 40 for those who have livestock.

Understanding the Form

For a form to get widespread acceptance, its flow and calculation logic should be apparent to the zakāt payers so that they can use the form with comfort and confidence that the form will assess zakāt with reasonable accuracy. It is for this reason that the form is accompanied by text discussing the principles of zakāt calculation on various assets in the chapter "Basic Principles of Assessing Zakāt". If this section is carefully read by the zakāt payer, then we believe that he or she will understand the underlying reasons for the layout of the form and its flow of logic.

Four Points to Keep in Mind

To understand the zakāt form (specifically the "comprehensive" form), the zakāt payer should bear in mind the following four important points:

1. *Different Assets*: There are four types of assets that the form calculates zakāt on: (1) money, (2) jewelry and gold, (3) trading goods, and (4) agricultural produce. Each of these assets has its own *niṣāb*. The *sharīʿa* does not approve of these assets being added together and then the sum being compared with *niṣāb*. Each of these should be compared with its own *niṣāb* before zakāt can be imposed on it. (For further discussion, see *Niṣāb* on page 46.)
2. *Sources of Money:* The asset "money" has four sources in the form: savings, earned income, business income, and shares and bonds. For the purpose of zakāt calculation, these are all considered the same type of asset: "money". Therefore, once their net value is calculated, they are added together (in the "Money" section) and then the result is compared with *niṣāb* for money to see if zakāt is due on money.
3. *Applying Deduction*: Before an asset is compared with *niṣāb* to find if zakāt may be due on it, deduction should be applied against it if the zakāt payer has any deduction. Then the net result should be compared with *niṣāb* for that asset (see *Minimum Standard of Living* on page 43). Once the deduction is applied against an asset, that deduction cannot be used against another asset. But if the deduction was not fully applied, then the remainder of the deduction can be used against a second asset.

   To illustrate this, let us say that one has net zakātable money of $20,000 and agricultural produce of $10,000. His deduction was calculated to be $18,000. In this case, $18,000 deduction would be fully applied against the money making its net amount $2,000 ($20,000 - $18,000). This $2,000 will be compared with *niṣāb* for money. Since the deduction was fully used against money, no further deduction can be applied against $10,000 of agricultural produce. If, on the other hand, the zakāt payer had $15,000 of money, then the deduction would be applied as follows: out of $18,000 of available deduction, $15,000 would be applied against money (bringing it to $0) and the remaining $3,000 would be applied against agricultural produce bringing its value to $7,000 ($10,000 - $3,000).

4. *Zakāt on Money*: We have mentioned above that money has four sources. Deduction, therefore, should be applied against money after adding these four sources together, and then the resulting amount should be compared with *niṣāb*. Here, it should be understood that if after applying the deduction the resulting amount is less than the *niṣāb* on money, then there is no zakāt on any of the four sources. If it is at or above *niṣāb*, then there will be zakāt on these sources. In that case, the deduction that was applied against money should be *proportionately distributed* among these sources before zakāt can be assessed on them. This is to ensure the accuracy of the zakāt calculation, since the rate of zakāt on these four sources is not the same (zakāt rate on business is 10%, unlike savings, earned income, and shares and bonds where the rate is 2.5%).

If the above four points are kept in mind, then the zakāt payer should be able to understand the layout and flow of the form.

Line Numbers

Other than for referential purposes, the line numbers do not have any special significance. Why then, one would ask, have we not used sequential numbers, such as 1, 2, 3, and so on like we see in tax forms? We could have used simple sequential numbers, but the reason we have adopted this numbering algorithm, such as S1, S2, E1, E2, etc. is only to make the form simpler than what it would have been had we used sequential numbers. For example, "S" points to a line for savings section, while "B" points to one in business. Thus, if asked to refer to B20, the zakāt payer will know that this line belongs to the business section.

Additionally, we have attempted to put some consistency in the numbers to increase readability and to help the zakāt payer use the form with more ease. For example, on each section line 20 shows the zakātable amount for that particular asset before deduction and *niṣāb* is considered. E20 and B20, therefore, would point to net earned income and net business income, respectively, before deduction and *niṣāb* is considered. Similarly, E25 and B25 would show the final amount on which zakāt is due after deduction and *niṣāb* was considered.

This numbering algorithm should make the form better understood, and we believe that although it may appear cryptic at first look, the zakāt payer will soon realize the readability and easiness that this numbering algorithm provides.

One Limitation

We have mentioned above that the form calculates zakāt on four types of assets: money, jewelry and gold, trading goods, and agricultural produce. It will be noticed that the deduction is not proportionately distributed against these assets, but is sequentially distributed starting from money. In other words, the deduction is first applied against money if there is zakātable money. If there is still some deduction left, then the remaining deduction is applied against jewelry and gold if there is zakātable jewelry. Similarly, a further deduction is applied against trading goods, and then lastly to agricultural produce.

One may correctly argue that the deduction should be proportionately distributed against all zakātable assets based on the amounts of these assets and the available deduction amount. This was considered by us while developing the form, but although it may seem ideal to proportionately distribute the deduction, it would provide almost no additional accuracy in the zakāt calculation for the vast majority of zakāt payers but would only increase the complexity of the form. For, the zakāt payer would then have to calculate the net zakātable asset on each section, then proportionately distribute the deduction against all these sections, and then re-visit each section to calculate the net zakāt.

This additional complexity would not result in additional accuracy in the calculation of zakāt for the vast majority of zakāt payers for the reason that out of the four asset types, the first three types have the same *niṣāb* and zakāt rate (*niṣāb* is 85g of gold and the zakāt rate is 2.5% on money,[121] jewelry and gold, and trading goods). Only the last asset – agricultural produce – has a different *niṣāb* and zakāt rate. Very few zakāt payers, however, will have zakātable agricultural produce. Even for the few zakāt payers who may have agricultural produce, the current form will not likely make any significant difference in their zakāt calculation. If there is any such slight difference, then it will be in the form of additional zakāt which will benefit the poor and earn additional reward for the zakāt payer, and not underassessment of zakāt which will be an injustice to the poor and the needy.

It should be mentioned here that the form does distribute deduction proportionately against the four sources within the money asset, since one of these sources is business income that has a different zakāt rate than the other three sources. One might legitimately wonder why we have considered business income and applied the deduction proportionately against the sources of money, but did not consider agricultural produce and do the same proportionate distribution against it. The reason is that business income is much more common than agricultural produce for a typical city-dwelling modern man for whom this form is primarily designed.

Which Form Should I Use?

Two forms are provided with this book: (1) the "short" form, and (2) the "comprehensive" form. The short form is simpler and easier to use since it calculates zakāt only on savings and earned income. It can, therefore, be used only by those who have zakātable savings and/or earned income, and no other types of zakātable assets. The majority of the zakāt payers will be in this category. They can also choose to use the comprehensive form which will result in the same amount of zakāt, but the form is more complex to use.

Zakāt payers who have other types of zakātable assets in addition to savings and earned income, such as business income, shares and bonds, jewelry, trading goods, and agricultural produce, must use the comprehensive form to accurately calculate their zakāt.

The line numbers are used consistently in both forms, and so the instructions that are given to help the zakāt payer on certain line numbers (shown on page 82) are applicable for both forms. Also, both forms utilize the same tables that are shown on page 93, with the exception that the "Deduction Distribution Worksheet" is not used by the short form.

Zakāt Calculation – Short Form

Please Note: (1) This "short" form is applicable for those who have zakātable *savings and/or earned income only*. If you have other types of zakātable assets besides savings and earned income, such as gold and jewelry, business, trading goods, agriculture, etc. then you must use the "comprehensive" form on page 88. (2) Unless otherwise specified, "year" refers to the zakāt year, based on the lunar calendar, for which you are calculating zakāt. (3) The *Niṣāb* Table and the Deduction Table must be completed first before filling in the form. (4) Zakāt cannot be calculated jointly – each individual must fill in a separate form. (5) Round figures to whole digits – do not use decimals. Use of pencil recommended.

You can skip the "Savings" or the "Earned Income" section if you do not have any savings or earned income, respectively.

Name: ____________________

Zakāt Year	From	To
Hijra / CE	/	/
Prior Year-End Date (Subtract 1 day from above):		
Dependents:	☐ I am responsible for the living expenses of ___ people including myself ☐ My living expenses are the responsibility of another person	

SAVINGS

S1	Total savings including cash and bank accounts as of the prior year-end date (PYED)		S1	
S2	Any outstanding zakāt due for the previous zakāt year (ending on PYED)		S2	
S3	Subtract S2 from S1: Total savings prior to the beginning of the zakāt year		S3	
S4	Total savings including cash and bank accounts as of the current year-end date ("To" date)		S4	
S5	Enter the lesser of S3 and S4: Savings kept for one year		S5	
S6	Outstanding loans you made to others and expected to be paid back (*see instruction*)		S6	
S20	Add S5 and S6: Total zakātable savings (pre-deduction and pre-*niṣāb*)		S20	

EARNED INCOME

E1	Total gross wage during the year		E1	
E2	Alimony received during the year		E2	
E3	Unemployment compensation received during the year		E3	
E4	Social Security benefit received during the year		E4	
E5	Pension received during the year		E5	
E6	Add E1 thru E5: Total earned income		E6	
E7	Income taxes paid on the above		E7	
E8	Additional estimated taxes due on the above at the time of filing tax return		E8	
E9	Or, Estimated tax amount to be refunded due to overpayment		E9	
E10	Add E7 and E8, then subtract E9 from the result: Total taxes paid		E10	

E11	Alimony paid		**E11**	
E12	Any other non-voluntary deductions from the wages and income		**E12**	
E13	Add E10 thru E12: Total non-voluntary deductions		**E13**	
E20	Subtract E13 from E6: Net earned income (pre-deduction and pre-*niṣāb*)		**E20**	

FINAL

M20	Add S20 and E20: Total zakātable savings and earnings (pre-deduction and pre-*niṣāb*)		**M20**	
M21	Enter line 10 from the Deduction Table: Deduction available		**M21**	
M23	Subtract M21 from M20: Zakātable amount after deduction (pre-*niṣāb*)		**M23**	
F25	If M23 < NM in *Niṣāb* Table, enter $0 here, otherwise multiply M23 by 0.025: Zakāt due on		**F25**	
F26	Zakāt paid in advance throughout the year		**F26**	
F27	Subtract F26 from F25: Remaining zakāt due		**F27**	

Zakāt Calculation – Comprehensive Form

Please Note: (1) Unless otherwise specified, "year" refers to the zakāt year, based on the lunar calendar, for which you are calculating zakāt. (2) The *Niṣāb* Table and the Deduction Table must be completed first before filling in the form. (3) Zakāt cannot be calculated jointly – each individual must fill in a separate form. (4) Round figures to whole digits – do not use decimals. Use of pencil recommended.

Name: ______________________________

Zakāt Year	From	To
Hijra / CE	/	/
Prior Year-End Date (Subtract 1 day from above):		
Dependents:	☐ I am responsible for the living expenses of ___ people including myself ☐ My living expenses are the responsibility of another person	

SAVINGS

S1	Total savings including cash and bank accounts as of the prior year-end date (PYED)		**S1**	
S2	Any outstanding zakāt due for the previous zakāt year (ending on PYED)		**S2**	
S3	Subtract S2 from S1: Total savings prior to the beginning of the zakāt year		**S3**	
S4	Total savings including cash and bank accounts as of the current year-end date ("To" date) (*see instruction*)		**S4**	
S5	Enter the lesser of S3 and S4: Savings kept for one year		**S5**	
S6	Outstanding loans you made to others and expected to be paid back (*see instruction*)		**S6**	
S20	Add S5 and S6: Total zakātable savings (pre-deduction and pre-*niṣāb*)		**S20**	
	Skip the following 2 lines for now until the MONEY section is calculated			
S22	If M25 = $0 enter S20 here, otherwise do M22 x S20 / M20: Deduction/*niṣāb* applied		**S22**	
S25	Subtract S22 from S20: Zakāt is due on this amount		**S25**	

EARNED INCOME

E1	Total gross wage during the year		**E1**	
E2	Alimony received during the year		**E2**	
E3	Unemployment compensation received during the year		**E3**	
E4	Social Security benefit received during the year		**E4**	
E5	Pension received during the year		**E5**	
E6	Add E1 thru E5: Total earned income		**E6**	
E7	Income taxes paid on the above		**E7**	
E8	Additional estimated taxes due on the above at the time of filing tax return		**E8**	
E9	Or, Estimated tax amount to be refunded due to overpayment		**E9**	
E10	Add E7 and E8, then subtract E9 from the result: Total taxes paid		**E10**	
E11	Alimony paid		**E11**	
E12	Any other non-voluntary deductions from the wages and income		**E12**	
E13	Add E10 thru E12: Total non-voluntary deductions		**E13**	
E20	Subtract E13 from E6: Net earned income (pre-deduction and pre-*niṣāb*)		**E20**	
	Skip the following 2 lines for now until the MONEY section is calculated			
E22	If M25 = $0 enter E20 here, otherwise do M22 x E20 / M20: Deduction/*niṣāb* applied		**E22**	
E25	Subtract E22 from E20: Zakāt is due on this amount		**E25**	

BUSINESS

B1	Total revenue from business or rental property during the year		**B1**	
B2	Operating expenses (*see instruction*)		**B2**	
B3	Subtract B2 from B1: Net income		**B3**	
B4	Your share in the business (1.00 if 100%, 0.50 if 50%, etc. *see instructions*)		**B4**	
B20	Multiply B3 by B4: Net income from business (pre-deduction and pre-*niṣāb*)		**B20**	
	Skip the following 2 lines for now until the MONEY section is calculated			

B22	If M25 = $0 enter B20 here, otherwise do M22 x B20 / M20: Deduction/*niṣāb* applied		**B22**	
B25	Subtract B22 from B20: Zakāt is due on this amount		**B25**	

SHARES

H1	Value of shares and bonds* you owned as of the end of the previous zakāt year (PYED)		**H1**	
H2	Value of shares and bonds you owned as of the end date of the current zakāt year ("To" date)		**H2**	
H3	Enter the lesser of H1 and H2: Value of shares and bonds kept for one year		**H3**	
H4	Dividends earned on shares during the zakāt year (excluding re-investments). *See instruction.*		**H4**	
H5	Add H3 and H4: Total value and earnings from shares and bonds		**H5**	
H6	Associated expenses including estimated income tax due on earnings and capital gains		**H6**	
H20	Subtract H6 from H5: Net value of shares and stocks (pre-deduction and pre-*niṣāb*)		**H20**	
	Skip the following 2 lines for now until the MONEY section is calculated			
H22	If M25 = $0 enter H20 here, otherwise do M22 x H20 / M20: Deduction/*niṣāb* applied		**H22**	
H25	Subtract H22 from H20: Zakāt is due on this amount		**H25**	

MONEY

M20	Add S20, E20, B20, and H20: Total of all money assets (pre-deduction and pre-*niṣāb*)		**M20**	
M21	Enter line DD from the DD Sheet: Deduction available		**M21**	
M22	Enter the lesser of M20 and M21 here and in line DM of DD Sheet: Deduction applied		**M22**	
M23	Subtract M22 from M20: Total money on which zakāt may be due (pre-*niṣāb*)		**M23**	
M25	If M23<NM in *Niṣāb* Table, enter $0 here, otherwise enter M23: Zakāt is due on this amount		**M25**	

* Bonds earn interest which is prohibited in Islam. See *Shares and Bonds* on page 53 for discussion about interest income. **Important:** Value of shares, bonds, jewelry, gold, and trading goods need to be determined as of certain dates. See instructions on those line items.

	Now complete Savings, Earned Income, Business, and Shares sections, then proceed below. (Note: If Jewelry, Business, Trading Goods and Agriculture sections are not applicable to you, you may choose to multiply M25 by 0.025, enter the result in F25, and complete the calculation.)			

JEWELRY

J1	Value of jewelry owned since the end of previous zakāt year (PYED) that is beyond customary use		**J1**	
J2	Value of other gold and gold assets (such as utensils) owned since the end of previous zakāt year		**J2**	
J20	Add J1 and J2: Value of zakātable gold and jewelry kept for one year (pre-deduction)		**J20**	
J21	Subtract line DM from line DD in the DD Sheet and enter here: Deduction available		**J21**	
J22	Enter the lesser of J20 and J21 here and also in line DJ: Deduction applied		**J22**	
J23	Subtract J22 from J20: Value of gold and jewelry on which zakāt may be due (pre-*niṣāb*)		**J23**	
J25	If J23 < Line NJ in *Niṣāb* Table, then enter $0 here, otherwise enter J23: Zakāt is due on this amount		**J25**	

TRADING GOODS

T1	Value of all trading goods (*see instruction*) owned at the end of previous zakāt year (PYED)		**T1**	
T2	Value of all trading goods owned at the end of the current zakāt year ("To" date)		**T2**	
T3	Enter the lesser of T1 and T2: Value of trading goods kept for one year		**T3**	
T4	Outstanding debts on the above assets (*see instruction*)		**T4**	
T20	Subtract T4 from T3: Net value of trading goods (pre-deduction)		**T20**	
T21	Subtract lines DM and DJ from line DD in the DD Sheet and enter here: Deduction available		**T21**	
T22	Enter the lesser of T20 and T21 here and also in line DT: Deduction applied		**T22**	

T23	Subtract T22 from T20: Value of trading goods on which zakāt may be due (pre-*niṣāb*)		**T23**	
T25	If T23 < line NT in *Niṣāb* Table, then enter $0 here, otherwise enter T23: Zakāt is due on this amount		**T25**	

AGRICULTURE

A1	Total value of all agricultural produce		**A1**	
A2	Cost of irrigation, fertilizer, labour and other operating expenses		**A2**	
A20	Subtract A2 from A1: Net value of agricultural produce (pre-deduction)		**A20**	
A21	Subtract lines DM, DJ and DT from DD in the DA Sheet and enter here: Deduction available		**A21**	
A22	Enter the lesser of A20 and A21 here and also in line DA: Deduction applied		**A22**	
A23	Subtract A22 from A20: Value of agricultural produce on which zakāt may be due (pre-*niṣāb*)		**A23**	
A25	If A23 < line NA in *Niṣāb* Table, then enter $0 here, otherwise enter A23: Zakāt is due on this amount		**A25**	

FINAL

F1	Multiply S25 by 0.025: Zakāt due on savings		**F1**	
F2	Multiply E25 by 0.025: Zakāt due on earned income		**F2**	
F3	Multiply B25 by 0.10: Zakāt due on business income		**F3**	
F4	Multiply H25 by 0.025: Zakāt due on shares and bonds		**F4**	
F5	Multiply J25 by 0.025: Zakāt due on gold, jewelry, and precious items		**F5**	
F6	Multiply T25 by 0.025: Zakāt due on trading goods		**F6**	
F7	Multiply A25 by 0.10 or 0.05 or 0.075 (see *instruction*): Zakāt due on agricultural produce		**F7**	
F25	Add lines F1 thru F7, or multiply M25 by 0.025 if applicable: Total zakāt due		**F25**	
F26	Zakāt paid in advance throughout the year		**F26**	
F27	Subtract F26 from F25: Remaining zakāt due		**F27**	

Tables and Worksheets

The *Niṣāb Table* and the *Deduction Table* must be completed first before using the zakāt form. The *Deduction Distribution Worksheet* is maintained while filling up the zakāt form.

Niṣāb Table

NIṢĀB				
NM	*Niṣāb* on money (value of 85g of gold)		NM	
NJ	*Niṣāb* on gold and jewelry (value of 85g of gold)		NJ	
NT	*Niṣāb* on trading goods (value of 85g of gold)		NT	
NA	*Niṣāb* on agricultural produce (value of 653kg of produce)		NA	

Determine the *niṣāb* on the above items before using the zakāt form. As of 3/13/2002, the value of 85g of gold was $800 at the rate $292.90 per ounce (1g = 0.03215 oz). Current US gold prices can be obtained at www.goldinfo.net. For discussion about *niṣāb* on agricultural produce, see *Agricultural Output* on page 26.

Deduction Table

DEDUCTIONS				
1	Cost of housing for a lunar year		1	
2	Cost of utilities for a lunar year		2	
3	Cost of transportation for a lunar year		3	
4	Cost of food and other basic necessities for a lunar year		4	
5	Actual Medical cost		5	
6	Add 1 thru 5: Standard deduction needed to fulfill the basic needs		6	
7	For all *necessary* debts *that are still outstanding*, the total original loan amount		7	
8	Total amounts paid so far		8	
9	Subtract 8 from 7: Your remaining zakāt exempt debt		9	
10	Add 6 and 9, and enter here and in line DD below: Total deduction		10	

A standard deduction amount that is needed to fulfill the basic necessities of the individual and his or her dependents should be agreed upon by the Islamic scholars or the *fiqh* council of the state or the area. If such an agreed-upon amount is not available, then this table may be used by the zakāt payer to calculate his or her standard deduction.

Lines 1–4: For cost of housing, utilities, transportation, food and other basic necessities, the amount needed to maintain the basic minimum standard for the zakāt payer and his/her dependents should be used, and not the actual cost which may be considerably higher. If the actual cost (during the zakāt year) happens to be less than the standard minimum cost, then the actual cost should be used. For example, the housing and utility cost will be $0 for a wife whose needs are provided for by her husband. The cost for a lunar year can be calculated by multiplying the cost for a Gregorian (solar) year by 0.967.

Line 5: For medical costs that are deemed necessary, use the actual amount spent. Do not include the premium for medical insurance if you have already subtracted it from your earnings (in line E12).

Line 7: Do not include business debts or debts that have already been paid. Business debts will be considered when calculating zakāt on business income and trading goods. Short-term credit card balance due to day-to-day charges for food and basic necessities should not be included as "debt" since standard deduction already includes the cost of basic necessities. To be exempt from zakāt, debt should be due to necessity and only that portion of the loan amount should be considered the "original loan amount" that is below the limit of extravagance. For instance, if one buys a house for $500,000 while the price of a mediocre house is $200,000 in a certain area, then $200,000 should be considered the "loan amount". See *"Debt"* on page 31 for more discussion.

Line 8: All payments should be considered as applied towards the original loan amount.

Deduction Distribution Worksheet (DD Sheet)

DEDUCTION DISTRIBUTION				
DD	Enter line 10 from above: Total deduction available		**DD**	
DM	Deduction applied against money assets (from the MONEY section, line M22)		**DM**	
DJ	Deduction applied against jewelry (from the JEWELRY section, line J22)		**DJ**	
DT	Deduction applied against trading goods (from the TR GOODS section, line T22)		**DT**	
DA	Deduction applied against agricultural produce (from the AGRI section, line A22)		**DA**	

Instructions

Instructions are provided only for those line items that are likely to require clarification.

Zakāt Year

Establish your zakāt year. Many Muslims calculate zakāt during Ramaḍān for the added reward of worshipping during this blessed month. So, an example of the zakāt year may be from Ramaḍān 11, 1421 to Ramaḍān 10, 1422. Since these dates are important in the calculation of zakāt, it would be preferable not to use the first or the last day of the month in the date range for the zakāt year due to the variability of number of days in the lunar month. Once a zakāt year is established, the same date range should be used for future zakāt years.

Savings

S1-S2: Find your total cash and bank balances you had as of the last day of the previous zakāt year (PYED), which is one day prior to the beginning of the current zakāt year. This would be the amount – after subtracting the past year's zakāt due – that you likely have kept throughout the zakāt year, unless it has been reduced later.

S4: Find your total cash and bank balances as of the last day of the current zakāt year ("To" date) for which you are calculating zakāt.

Your bank balance should also include any uninvested cash that is available in your stockbroker account.

S5: The lesser of S3 and S4 is the actual savings amount that you have kept throughout the zakāt year.

S6: Include outstanding loan amounts that people owe to you and are expected to be paid. Do not include any loan that originated during the zakāt year, that is on or after the start date of the current zakāt year (the "From" date). Also, do not include loans and credits owed to your business.

S20: This is your zakātable savings before any consideration for *niṣāb* or deduction for minimum living standard, which will be considered after combining all liquid money assets together in the *Money* section.

S22: M25 represents the zakātable amount of all the four money assets (*Savings, Earned Income, Business,* and *Shares*) together. If it is zero, then no zakāt is due on these money assets. In that case, the entire money in S20 is deductible; hence S20 should be entered in S22 to offset the amount. If M25 is greater than zero, then calculate the proportionate amount of deduction to be applied here against zakātable savings by multiplying M22 (total deduction for money) by S20 (zakātable savings) and dividing the result by M20 (total of all four money assets).

Earned Income

E1-E5: Only those earnings should be included that occurred during the zakāt year – between the "From" and the "To" date in the form. It is recommended that the "pay date" on the cheque stub be used in determining which earnings fall in the zakāt year. Cash earnings (such as tips) should be included based on when the cash was received.

If you are self-employed and receive a salary from your business, then include that as well.

Do not include non-earned income here, such as profit from business, rent income, earnings from shares, etc. These will be calculated in separate sections.

E7-E9: Taxes should be taken out from the gross income, since zakāt is due on the net amount only. For further discussion on this, see *Net Earnings vs. Gross Earnings* on page 44.

The tax amount should be adjusted in consideration of additional taxes due or refund due during the time of the tax return. This can only be estimated since the zakāt year will likely not synchronize with the tax year, which will include a different set of earnings.

E12: Non-voluntary deductions, such as income tax, Social Security and Medicare deductions should be deducted from the gross income. Pension contribution is a voluntary deduction, hence it is not included. Health insurance deduction is also non-voluntary. However, in our opinion, this may be considered as a medical expense when calculating standard deductions on page 95.

E20: This shows the net zakātable earnings before any consideration for *niṣāb* or deduction for minimum living standard, which will be considered after combining all liquid money assets together in the *Money* section.

E22: See S22 for explanation.

Business Income

B1: If you have a business, then include all revenue made *during* the zakāt year. If you receive rent from rental properties, include also the rents you received *during* the zakāt year.

If you have business merchandise and trading goods, then zakāt on those will be calculated separately in the *Trading Goods* section. For discussion about zakāt on business, see *Business* on page 27.

B2: Include all business expenses, such as payroll, rent, utility, taxes, supplies, merchandise, amortization, and bad debts that occurred *during* the zakāt year. If the exact amount is not known for an item, use a reasonable estimate. If you received salary from your business, then include that as part of the payroll expenses. Also include estimated income taxes that you will have to pay on the net income, if any, from these specific earnings that are included here.

If you received rent from rental properties, then include all associated expenses, such as repairs, insurance, loan payments, property tax, and estimated income tax on the rent.

B4: If you have several businesses with different amounts of shares in them, then do B1 thru B4 for each business to calculate the net income separately. Then add all the net income together, subtract estimated income taxes, and enter the result in B20.

B22: See S22 for explanation.

Shares and Bonds

H1: Include only those shares and bonds that you owned on the last day of the previous zakāt year (PYED), and use the market value as of that date. Purchases made during this year should not be included in this. See *Determining the Value of a Given Asset* on page 30 about assessing the value of shares and bonds.

H2: Include all shares and bonds that you owned on the last day of the current zakāt year ("To" date), and use the market value as of that date.

H3: The lesser of H1 and H3 is the value of shares and bonds that you have maintained for one year, which is subject to zakāt. For further discussion, see *Shares and Bonds* on page 53.

H4: Include only those earnings that occurred within the zakāt year. If any part of the earning was re-invested into purchasing stocks or bonds during the zakāt year, then exclude that portion from the earning. This is to avoid duplication of zakāt since line H2 already includes the value of all stocks and bonds.

H6: Include all associated expenses, including estimated income tax on earnings and capital gains.

H22: See S22 for explanation.

Money

This section adds together all the zakātable liquid money assets that were determined in the *Savings, Earned Income, Business*, and *Shares* sections. After subtracting the necessary deductions, if the total sum reaches *niṣāb* on money, then zakāt is due on money. In that case, zakāt will be calculated on each of these money assets separately (since the rate of zakāt on these assets varies) after proportionately distributing the available deduction amount against these assets.

M20: Add together all the zakātable money assets that were determined in the *Savings, Earned Income, Business* and *Shares* sections.

M21: Get the total deduction available from line DD of the Deduction Distribution Worksheet (*DD Sheet*) on page 95.

M22: The lesser of the asset (M20) and the available deduction amount (M21) is the actual deduction that is applied against the asset. Enter this amount in M22 and also in line DM of the *DD Sheet* on page 95.

M25: After subtracting the deduction from the total gross zakātable money, what is left is subject to zakāt. Compare this with the *niṣāb* for money shown in the *Niṣāb Table* on page 93. If it is less than *niṣāb*, then no zakāt is due on any of the four money assets, i.e., *Savings, Earned Income, Business*, and *Shares*.

Note: If you are calculating zakāt on *Savings, Earned Income*, and *Shares* only (i.e., *Jewelry, Business, Trading Goods*, and *Agricultural* sections are not applicable to you), then you can choose to complete your calculation now by multiplying M25 by 0.025 and skipping to F25. Or you can continue if you like. In both cases, your zakāt will be the same.

Jewelry

J1: Include any jewelry that is beyond customary use within your social status, since what is subject to zakāt is the jewelry that is extravagant or kept as stored wealth, not the jewelry that is for personal use. Precious stones, such as diamonds, are also included if they are beyond customary use. Men are prohibited to wear golden or precious jewelry; hence their entire jewelry is subject to zakāt.

Only that jewelry should be included that is owned since the prior year-end date, and use the market value as of the current year-end date.

J2: This includes all gold and gold-made items owned since the prior year-end date. Use the market value as of the current year-end date.

J21-J22: After subtracting the deduction already applied against money (DM) from the total available deduction (DD), what is left is the available deduction (J21). The lesser of this and the value of zakātable gold and jewelry (J20) is the actual deduction that can be applied against this asset. Enter this amount in J22 and also in line DJ of the *DD Sheet* on page 95.

Trading Goods

T1: Trading goods include any economic good or property that is intended for resale, such as business inventory, real estate property, machinery, clothing, foodstuff, etc. Fixed assets that are not for sale but are utilized by the business to generate revenue are not considered trading goods.

Enter the estimated value of the trading goods that you owned on the prior year-end date. Use the market value as of the prior year-end date. See *Determining the Value of a Given Asset* on page 30 for assessing the value of trading goods.

T2: Enter the estimated value of trading goods that you own as of the current year-end date, and use the market value as of that date.

T3: The lesser of T1 and T2 is the value of trading goods that you have maintained for one year, which is subject to zakāt. For more discussion, see *Business Goods and Business Income* on page 27.

T4: Enter all outstanding debts against the trading goods. Do not include any debt that has already been included in the Deduction Table.

T21-T22: After subtracting the deduction already applied against money (DM) and jewelry (DJ) from the total available deduction (DD), what is left is the available deduction (T21). The lesser of this and the value of zakātable trading goods (T20) is the actual deduction that can be applied against this asset. Enter this amount in T22 and also in line DT of the *DD Sheet* on page 95.

Agriculture

A1-A2: If you sharecrop, then include only the portion of the produce owned by you. Similarly, include only those expenses that are paid by you.

A21-A22: After subtracting the deduction already applied against money (DM), jewelry (DJ), and trading goods (DT) from the total available deduction (DD), what is left is the available deduction

(A21). The lesser of this and the value of zakātable agricultural produce (A20) is the actual deduction that can be applied against this asset. Enter this amount in A22 and also in line DA of the *DD Sheet* on page 95.

Final Calculation

F1-F6: Zakāt on savings, earned income, shares and bonds, gold, jewelry, and trading goods is 2.5%. On business income including rent, zakāt is 10% of the net income.

F7: If the land was watered by rain all or most of the year, zakāt is 10%. If it was watered by irrigation mostly, zakāt is 5%. If the land was watered by rain and irrigation about equally then zakāt is 7.5%. See *Agricultural Output* on page 26 for further discussion.

Preparing For Next Year's Zakāt Calculation

Zakāt calculation at the end of the year can be made both easy and joyful by doing certain preparations during the year. These preparations include the following two main areas:

Keeping Track of Records

Calculating zakāt requires a lot of information, as should be evident by now to anyone who has attempted to use the zakāt form. Not having this information available when calculating zakāt makes it difficult to use the form and calculate zakāt accurately. In order to calculate next year's zakāt in less time and more accurately, the following is suggested to the zakāt payer:

- The zakāt payer should save the current year's zakāt calculation form and supporting worksheets. The form will provide much valuable information when calculating zakāt next year. For instance, line S4 from the current year's form will go into line S1 of next year's. Likewise, lines H2, T2, and F27 will go into lines H1, T1, and S2, respectively. In addition, the current form will provide other useful information and references in regard to loans, debts, and standard deduction amount, though these amounts may be different during next year.
- The zakāt payer should maintain a ledger and record any information in it that will be needed to complete the form next year. For example, any time the zakāt payer receives earnings, he should write down the pay date, gross amount, and taxes and other deductions paid. Other information that should be tracked besides earnings are: (1) Loans given out to others, (2) Amounts borrowed from others (debts), (3) Payments made towards debts, (4) Value of shares and bonds as of the zakāt end date of each zakāt year, (5) Dividends earned and expenses paid, (6) Medical expenses, and (7) Zakāt paid in advance throughout the year. It is important to record the dates of each transaction since transactions belonging to the specific zakāt year are included in the zakāt calculation. Appendix B shows a sample ledger showing entries that would be needed by the zakāt form.

Setting Aside Money to Pay Zakāt

In this present age people have an endless number of needs and priorities. Many of the amenities and services that were once considered luxuries have now become necessities. House, cars, cellular phones, computers, printers, investing for the future, retirement fund, children's needs, children's education fund, online service provider, entertainment, camera, TV, stereo, VCR, DVD player, cable network, multiple phone lines, satellite dish, camcorder, digital camera, new furniture, obligations to family and relatives – they all turn out to be priorities at some point. And as soon as existing priorities are met, new priorities arise. The result of this myriad of needs and priorities is that despite earning a substantial income, many people cannot retain a sufficient amount of money to pay zakāt that is due at the end of the zakāt year. Consequently, zakāt is delayed or not paid and thus this important obligation to Allah (swt) and to the poor remains unfulfilled.

One suggestion that can help an individual calculate and pay zakāt on time every year is to set aside a percentage of money that he or she earns during the year. One can set aside 3, 4, or 5% from every salary cheque and save it in a separate bank account designated for zakāt and charity. Thus at the end of the zakāt year, one will likely have sufficient money available to pay his zakāt without having to draw from his savings and current accounts. By making such conscious efforts and by giving such high priority to zakāt, one will soon develop a habit of calculating and paying zakāt on time every year. And since the money to pay zakāt would already be available, he will, *inshā' Allāh*, start looking forward to the end of the zakāt year when he would enjoy calculating zakāt and distributing it to those who would greatly benefit from his money.

Notes

121. Except business income where the zakāt rate is 10%, which is addressed in the next paragraph.

APPENDIX ❖ A

Sample Zakāt Calculation ("Comprehensive")

Name: DANIEL M. STROHMIER

Zakāt Year	**From**	**To**
Hijra / CE	Ramaḍān 11, 1421/Dec 7, 2000	Ramaḍān 10, 1422/Nov 26, 2001
Prior Year-End Date (Subtract 1 day from above)		Ramaḍān 10, 1421/Dec 6, 2000
Dependents:	☒ I am responsible for the living expenses of 4 people including myself ☐ My living expenses are the responsibility of another person	

SAVINGS				
S1	Total savings including cash and bank accounts as of the prior year-end date (PYED)	$9,700	**S1**	
S2	Any outstanding zakāt due for the previous zakāt year (ending on PYED)		**S2**	
S3	Subtract S2 from S1: Total savings prior to the beginning of the zakāt year		**S3**	$9,700
S4	Total savings including cash and bank accounts as of the current year-end date ("To" date) (*see instruction*)		**S4**	$12,100
S5	Enter the lesser of S3 and S4: Savings kept for one year	$9,700	**S5**	
S6	Outstanding loans you made to others and expected to be paid back (*see instruction*)	$500	**S6**	
S20	Add S5 and S6: Total zakātable savings (pre-deduction and pre-*niṣāb*)		**S20**	$10,200
	Skip the following 2 lines for now until the MONEY section is calculated			

S22	If M25 = $0 enter S20 here, otherwise do M22 x S20 / M20: Deduction/*niṣāb* applied		**S22**	$10,200
S25	Subtract S22 from S20: Zakāt is due on this amount		**S25**	$0

EARNED INCOME

E1	Total gross wage during the year	$40,000	**E1**	
E2	Alimony received during the year	$0	**E2**	
E3	Unemployment compensation received during the year	$0	**E3**	
E4	Social Security benefit received during the year	$0	**E4**	
E5	Pension received during the year	$0	**E5**	
E6	Add E1 thru E5: Total earned income		**E6**	$40,000
E7	Income taxes paid on the above	$10,000	**E7**	
E8	Additional estimated taxes due on the above at the time of filing tax return	$0	**E8**	
E9	Or, Estimated tax amount to be refunded due to overpayment	$1,200	**E9**	
E10	Add E7 and E8, then subtract E9 from the result: Total taxes paid	$8,800	**E10**	
E11	Alimony paid	$0	**E11**	
E12	Any other non-voluntary deductions from the wages and income	$0	**E12**	
E13	Add E10 thru E12: Total non-voluntary deductions		**E13**	$8,800
E20	Subtract E13 from E6: Net earned income (pre-deduction and pre-*niṣāb*)		**E20**	$31,200
	Skip the following 2 lines for now until the MONEY section is calculated			
E22	If M25 = $0 enter E20 here, otherwise do M22 x E20 / M20: Deduction/*niṣāb* applied		**E22**	$31,200
E25	Subtract E22 from E20: Zakāt is due on this amount		**E25**	$0

BUSINESS

B1	Total revenue from business or rental property during the year	$210,000	**B1**	
B2	Operating expenses (*see instruction*)	$185,000	**B2**	
B3	Subtract B2 from B1: Net income		**B3**	$25,000
B4	Your share in the business (1.00 if 100%, 0.50 if 50%, etc. *see instructions*)	$1.00	**B4**	

B20	Multiply B3 by B4: Net income from business (pre-deduction and pre-*niṣāb*)		**B20**	$25,000
	Skip the following 2 lines for now until the MONEY section is calculated			
B22	If M25 = $0 enter B20 here, otherwise do M22 x B20 / M20: Deduction/*niṣāb* applied		**B22**	$25,000
B25	Subtract B22 from B20: Zakāt is due on this amount		**B25**	$0

SHARES

H1	Value of shares and bonds* you owned as of the end of the previous zakāt year (PYED)	$5,000	**H1**	
H2	Value of shares and bonds you owned as of the end date of the current zakāt year ("To" date)	$7,500	**H2**	
H3	Enter the lesser of H1 and H2: Value of shares and bonds kept for one year	$5,000	**H3**	
H4	Dividends earned on shares during the zakāt year (excluding re-investments). *See instruction.*	$200	**H4**	
H5	Add H3 and H4: Total value and earning from shares and bonds		**H5**	$5,200
H6	Associated expenses including estimated income tax due on earnings and capital gains		**H6**	$60
H20	Subtract H6 from H5: Net value of shares and stocks (pre-deduction and pre-*niṣāb*)		**H20**	$5,140
	Skip the following 2 lines for now until the MONEY section is calculated			
H22	If M25 = $0 enter H20 here, otherwise do M22 x H20 / M20: Deduction/*niṣāb* applied		**H22**	$5,140
H25	Subtract H22 from H20: Zakāt is due on this amount		**H25**	$0

MONEY

M20	Add S20, E20, B20, and H20: Total of all money assets (pre-deduction and pre-*niṣāb*)		**M20**	$71,540
M21	Enter line DD from the DD Sheet: Deduction available	$72,400	**M21**	
M22	Enter the lesser of M20 and M21 here and in line DM of DD Sheet: Deduction applied		**M22**	$71,540
M23	Subtract M22 from M20: Total money on which zakāt may be due (pre-*niṣāb*)		**M23**	$0

* Bonds earn interest which is prohibited in Islam. See *Shares and Bonds* on page 53 for discussion about interest income. **Important:** Value of shares, bonds, jewelry, gold, and trading goods need to be determined as of certain dates. See instructions on those line items.

M25	If M23 < NM in *Niṣāb* Table, enter $0 here, otherwise enter M23: Zakāt is due on this amount		**M25**	$0
	Now complete Savings, Earned Income, Business, and Shares sections, then proceed below. (Note: If Jewelry, Business, Tr Goods and Agri. sections are not applicable to you, you may choose to multiply M25 by 0.025, enter the result in F25, and complete the calculation.)			

JEWELRY

J1	Value of jewelry owned since the end of previous zakāt year (PYED) that is beyond customary use	$1,000	**J1**	
J2	Value of other gold and gold assets (such as utensils) owned since the end of previous zakāt year	$0	**J2**	
J20	Add J1 and J2: Value of zakātable gold and jewelry kept for one year (pre-deduction)		**J20**	$1,000
J21	Subtract line DM from line DD in the DD Sheet and enter here: Deduction available	$860	**J21**	
J22	Enter the lesser of J20 and J21 here and also in line DJ: Deduction applied		**J22**	$860
J23	Subtract J22 from J20: Value of gold and jewelry on which zakāt may be due (pre-*niṣāb*)		**J23**	$140
J25	If J23 < Line NJ in *Niṣāb* Table, then enter $0 here, otherwise enter J23: Zakāt is due on this amount		**J25**	$0

TRADING GOODS

T1	Value of all trading goods (see *instruction*) owned at the end of previous zakāt year (PYED)	$205,000	**T1**	
T2	Value of all trading goods owned at the end of the current zakāt year ("To" date)	$200,000	**T2**	
T3	Enter the lesser of T1 and T2: Value of trading goods kept for one year	$200,000	**T3**	
T4	Outstanding debts on the above assets (see *instruction*)	$60,000	**T4**	

T20	Subtract T4 from T3: Net value of trading goods (pre-deduction)		**T20**	$140,000
T21	Subtract lines DM and DJ from line DD in the DD Sheet and enter here: Deduction available	$0	**T21**	
T22	Enter the lesser of T20 and T21 here and also in line DT: Deduction applied		**T22**	$0
T23	Subtract T22 from T20: Value of trading goods on which zakāt may be due (pre-*niṣāb*)		**T23**	$140,000
T25	If T23 < line NT in *Niṣāb* Table, then enter $0 here, otherwise enter T23: Zakāt is due on this amount		**T25**	$140,000

AGRICULTURE

A1	Total value of all agricultural produce	$100,000	**A1**	
A2	Cost of irrigation, fertilizer, labour and other operating expenses	$60,000	**A2**	
A20	Subtract A2 from A1: Net value of agricultural produce (pre-deduction)		**A20**	$40,000
A21	Subtract lines DM, DJ and DT from DD in the DA Sheet and enter here: Deduction available	$0	**A21**	
A22	Enter the lesser of A20 and A21 here and also in line DA: Deduction applied		**A22**	$0
A23	Subtract A22 from A20: Value of agricultural produce on which zakāt may be due (pre-*niṣāb*)		**A23**	$40,000
A25	If A23 < line NA in *Niṣāb* Table, then enter $0 here, otherwise enter A23: Zakāt is due on this amount		**A25**	$40,000

FINAL

F1	Multiply S25 by 0.025: Zakāt due on savings	$0	**F1**	
F2	Multiply E25 by 0.025: Zakāt due on earned income	$0	**F2**	
F3	Multiply B25 by 0.10: Zakāt due on business income	$0	**F3**	
F4	Multiply H25 by 0.025: Zakāt due on shares and bonds	$0	**F4**	

F5	Multiply J25 by 0.025: Zakāt due on gold, jewelry, and precious items	$0	**F5**	
F6	Multiply T25 by 0.025: Zakāt due on trading goods	$3,500	**F6**	
F7	Multiply A25 by 0.10 or 0.05 or 0.075 (see *instruction*): Zakāt due on agricultural produce	$4,000	**F7**	
F25	Add lines F1 thru F7, or multiply M25 by 0.025 if applicable: Total zakāt due		**F25**	$7,500
F26	Zakāt paid in advance throughout the year		**F26**	$2,500
F27	Subtract F26 from F25: Remaining zakāt due		**F27**	$5,000

Tables and Worksheets

Niṣāb Table

NIṢĀB				
NM	*Niṣāb* on money (value of 85g of gold)	$800	**NM**	
NJ	*Niṣāb* on gold and jewelry (value of 85g of gold)	$800	**NJ**	
NT	*Niṣāb* trading goods (value of 85g of gold)	$800	**NT**	
NA	*Niṣāb* on agricultural produce (value of 653kg of produce)		**NA**	

Deduction Table

DEDUCTION				
1	Cost of housing for a lunar year	$7,200	**1**	
2	Cost of utilities for a lunar year	$2,400	**2**	
3	Cost of transportation for a lunar year	$3,600	**3**	
4	Cost of food and other basic necessities for a lunar year	$6,000	**4**	
5	Actual Medical cost	$1,200	**5**	
6	Add 1 thru 5: Standard deduction needed to fulfill basic needs		**6**	$19,400
7	For all *necessary* debts *that are still outstanding*, the total original loan amount	$128,000	**7**	
8	Total amounts paid so far	$75,000	**8**	
9	Subtract 8 from 7: Your remaining zakāt exempt debt		**9**	$53,000
10	Add 6 and 9, and enter here and in line DD below: Total deduction		**10**	$72,400

Deduction Distribution Worksheet (DD Sheet)

DEDUCTION DISTRIBUTION				
DD	Enter line 10 from above: Total deduction available		**DD**	$72,400
DM	Deduction applied against money assets *(from the MONEY section, line M22)*	$71,540	**DM**	
DJ	Deduction applied against jewelry *(from the JEWELRY section, line J22)*	$860	**DJ**	
DT	Deduction applied against trading goods *(from the TR GOODS section, line T22)*	$0	**DT**	
DA	Deduction applied against agricultural produce *(from the AGRI section, line A22)*	$0	**DA**	

APPENDIX ❖ B

Sample Ledger for Recording Information

Below is a sample ledger showing information that is recorded during the year in preparation for the calculation of zakāt for the next zakāt year beginning, for example, on Ramaḍān 11, 1422 (11/27/2001) and ending on Ramaḍān 10, 1423 (11/15/2002).

Date	Description	Amount
11/26/01	Balance of personal savings, current, and cash accounts	$12,100
11/27/01	– Ramaḍān 11, 1422: Beginning of the new zakāt year –	
11/30/01	Salary – gross amount	$4,000
	Taxes paid	$1,000
12/10/01	Gave loan to Hasan	$2,500
12/28/01	Borrowed for purchase of car	$10,000
12/28/01	Payment against loan on car	$500
12/31/01	Salary – gross amount	$4,000
	Taxes paid	$1,000
01/20/02	Zakāt paid in advance	$75
01/31/02	Salary – gross amount	$4,000
	Taxes paid	$1,000
02/01/02	Payment against car loan	$500
02/07/02	Doctor's fee and prescription cost	$150
02/13/02	Purchased 300 RBAK shares	$1,500
	Broker fee	$20
02/28/02	Salary – gross amount	$4,000

	Taxes paid	$1,000
03/15/02	Prescription cost	$35
03/25/02	Zakāt paid in advance	$25
....	....	....
....	....	....
11/15/02	Balance of savings, current and cash accounts as of today	$8,000
11/15/02	Value of jewelry and gold as of today	$1,000
11/15/02	Value of shares and bonds as of today	$6,000
11/15/02	– Ramaḍān 10, 1423: End of the zakāt year –	

It would be useful to mark the last day of your zakāt year on your calendar and remind yourself to check the market value of shares, bonds, and other zakātable properties you may have as of that date. If you use an electronic calendar, then you can place a reminder in your electronic organizer or software to check the market prices.

These little preparations will not only help in the accuracy of your zakāt calculation but will also save time by providing the necessary information when you sit down to calculate your zakāt.

Index

"My Mercy extends to all things. That (Mercy) I shall ordain for those who do right and practise zakāt, and those who believe in Our Signs." – Qur'ān 7:156

"Wealth never decreases due to charity." – Prophet Muḥammad (peace be upon him)

"The institution of zakāt represents the foundation of a caring, sympathetic and supportive society, which has no cause to resort to usury in any aspect of its life." – Sayyid Quṭb, *In the Shade of the Qur'ān*

"... the contrast becomes clearer between the Islamic way and the capitalist way. Capitalists urge people to accumulate wealth and to collect interest on it so that they acquire more of other people's wealth. This is not consistent with the nature of this religion. Islam commands that if wealth happens to accumulate in your hands, it must flow through the channels of distribution provided by Islam so that life flourishes around you." – Sayyid Mawdūdī, *Economic Foundations in Islam Compared to Other Contemporary Systems*

"Although all that you possess is a gift from Him and belongs to Him alone, and although whatever you spend you spend on your own families, relatives, communities, or on your collective well-being, and not on Him, He nevertheless says: 'You have given it to Me, I will return it to you.'" – Sayyid Mawdūdī, *Let Us Be Muslims*

"The voice of Divinely revealed religions in calling for the care of the poor and weak has been even louder than other religious systems, having a deeper effect than any human philosophy or man-made law. I cannot believe any Messenger of Allah has passed through the world without calling for the care of the poor, called zakāt in the Qur'ān." – Yūsuf al-Qaraḍāwī, *Fiqh uz-Zakāt*

"Islam is unprecedented in the extent of its care for the poor and in its determination to solve the problem of poverty whether through directives and recommendations that exhort Muslims to show mercy to the poor, through legislation and laws, or through implementations and application." – Yūsuf al-Qaraḍāwī, *Fiqh uz-Zakāt*